Joseph Marshall

Travels through Holland, Flanders, Germany, Denmark, Sweden, Lapland, Russia, the Ukraine and Poland in the Years 1768, 1769 and 1770

Vol. 3

Joseph Marshall

Travels through Holland, Flanders, Germany, Denmark, Sweden, Lapland, Russia, the Ukraine and Poland in the Years 1768, 1769 and 1770
Vol. 3

ISBN/EAN: 9783337350918

Printed in Europe, USA, Canada, Australia, Japan

Cover: Foto ©Andreas Hilbeck / pixelio.de

More available books at **www.hansebooks.com**

TRAVELS

THROUGH

HOLLAND, LAPLAND,
FLANDERS, RUSSIA,
GERMANY, The UKRAINE,
DENMARK, AND
SWEDEN, POLAND,

IN THE

Years 1768, 1769, and 1770.

In which is particularly Minuted,

The PRESENT STATE

OF

THOSE COUNTRIES,

RESPECTING THEIR

AGRICULTURE, POPULATION,
MANUFACTURES, COMMERCE,
The ARTS, and USEFUL UNDERTAKINGS.

By JOSEPH MARSHALL, Esq;

VOL. III.

LONDON:
Printed for J. ALMON, opposite Burlington House,
Piccadilly.
MDCCLXXII.

CONTENTS of Vol. III.

Travels through Sweden, continued.

CHAP. I. *Journey from Lindſal to Hudwickſwald--- The Country, and the Huſbandry carried on by the Peaſants--Horſten--Deſcription of M. de Verſpot's fine Seat at Raverſburg---An Account of his very ſpirited Improvements.*

CHAP. II. *Hernoſand---Pleaſing Adventure with a Swediſh Peaſant---Huſbandry---Uma---State of Commerce---Pitha---Deſcription of the Country---Torneo---State of the Country in Eaſt Bothnia---Admirable Management of a Farmer---A Swediſh Club---Remarkable Country---Nyſtot---Wyburg.*

CHAP. III. *General Reflections on the State of Sweden---Religion---Learning---The fine Arts---Manner of Life---Government---Agriculture---Manufactures---Commerce---Wealth---Population---Travelling.*

Travels through Ruſſia.

CHAP. IV. *Deſcription of Peterſburg---General Accounts of the Empire of Ruſſia---The Empreſs---Government----Manufactures----Trade----Army---Navy---Preſent State.*

CHAP. V. *Journey from Peterſburg to Moſcow---Deſcription of the Country---Great Settlement of Poles---Moſcow---Journey into the Ukraine---Account of that fine Province---Deſcription of the Agriculture of it---Culture of Hemp, Tobacco, &c.*

CHAP,

CONTENTS.

CHAP. VI. *Journey to Peterſburg through the Frontiers of Poland---Obſervations on the State of ſeveral Provinces---Ruſſian Acquiſitions---Remarks on the War between the Ruſſians and the Turks---Journey to Archangel, and through Lapland---Return to Peterſburg---Livonia.*

Travels through Poland and Pruſſia.

CHAP. VII. *Journey to Dantzick---Deſcription of the Country and Huſbandry--Trade of Dantzick--Journey to Warſaw--Miſerable State of Poland---To Breſlaw.*

Travels through Germany.

CHAP. VIII. *Sileſia---Breſlaw--Journey to Berlin--The Country--Agriculture--Deſcription of Berlin--Preſent State of the King of Pruſſia's Forces, Revenues, &c.---Saxony--Leipſick--Dreſden--State of the Electorate.*

CHAP. IX. *Journey acroſs Bohemia--Prague---Deſcription of the Country---The People---Nobility--Huſbandry--Manufactures---Moravia---Olmutz--Brinn---Journey to Vienna---Deſcription of the Capital.*

CHAP. X. *Journey from Vienna through Auſtria---Deſcription of the Archdutchy---Bavaria---Munich---Revenues and Forces.*

Travels

Travels through Sweden,

Continued.

VOL. III.

CHAP. I.

Journey from Lindfal to Hudwickfwald—The Country, and the Hufbandry carried on by the Peafants—Horften—Defcription of M. de Verfpot's fine Seat at Raverfburg—An Account of his very fpirited Improvements.

IT was the evening of the 28th of June before I arrived at Lindfal, which is a little inconfiderable village. From thence I fet out the next morning for Hudwickfwald, the diftance fixty miles, which proved a journey of two days. The night of the 1ft I laid at Dilfbo; the country very wild and mountainous, like Dalecarlia, and not better cultivated: in fome of the vales are fmall villages, the inhabitants of fome of which have little farms, but I do not think are quite fo induftrious in their management of them as their neighbours of Dalecarnia. Dilfbo ftands on a river near the Baltic, and has a harbour that admits fhips of two hundred tons burthen, but yet there is hardly any trade at it: now and then a veffel comes for a load of timber, but it is feldom. From thence to Hud-

Hudwickfwald is through a flat country, pretty well cultivated, and the inhabitants much more induſtrious. I ſaw two or three large houſes, ſurrounded by conſiderable farms; gentlemen's ſeats; and the owners ſeem to carry on a husbandry equal to any thing I have ſeen in Sweden in general. I found their crops generally good; and the products riſe, upon a medium of all ſorts, to three or four quarters per acre: their dwarf beans are a favourite crop here, for I ſaw many fields of them: they do not grow more than a foot high. Another thing I found here, of which I had ſeen little before, which was, great plenty of trefoile; it is a ſort not common in England, tho' the bloſſom is yellow; they ſow it among their corn, and for two or three years following mow or feed it; which appears to be the ſame ſyſtem as the culture of clover in England, and trefoile in England, and alſo ſainfoim. Artificial graſſes I have very rarely ſeen in this kingdom, and there is certainly a reaſon for it; the great plenty of wild ground and marſhes, on which the peaſants depend for the ſubſiſtence of their cattle.
—— Hudwickfwald is extremely well ſituated for the Baltic trade; the harbour is ſpacious, ſafe, and admits ſhips of any burthen: there are a few merchants in the town, that are rich.

rich. They have a tolerable quay; they shewed me the church which is usually exhibited to strangers, but contains not the least thing worthy of observation. Most of the streets are regular, clean, and some of them very neatly built.

Here I made enquiries after M. de Verspot, and found, after some difficulty, that I must take the road north to a village called Tuna, and from thence follow a road which runs westward near the river on which Tuna stands, and in about five or six and thirty miles I should come to a place called Horsten, near which that gentleman's seat is.

The first of July I got to Tuna, the distance from Hudwickswald thirty-six miles. The country is various; parts of it marshy, and parts dry: a good deal of the latter is cultivated, but I saw no gentlemen's houses. I found that many of the peasants here paid their rents in parts of the products of their land, and that their landlords stewards came in sloops from Stockholm at a certain time of the year, to receive these products: this is reckoned here very advantageous to the landlords, for they have the corn, &c. at a much less calculated value than what they sell it for at Stockholm, all expences reckoned; but at the same time, the peasants like it better than being forced to find the money, which is very scarce here. They cultivate large quantities of corn, and many turneps and carrots; and have the art of fattening oxen with these roots in winter, by boiling and mashing them, and then mixing some meal of barley or oats with them: with this food their oxen and their hogs fatten very quickly, and they reckon, if the crop of roots is good, it proves, in this way of using it, one of the best a farmer can cultivate. They do not use wood-ashes in this country, which is so principal a manure in most of the parts of Sweden through which I have passed, but depend totally on dung, which they mix up with earth, and think it thus exceeds any other manure that can be had. The dung of swine they reckon the most powerful.

I reached Horsten the 2d; and, fixing my bed in the house of a civil peasant, made enquiries after M. de Verspot. I was informed that he lived about eight miles from thence; that all Horsten belonged to him, and also many more villages in the neighbourhood:—that he had the greatest estate in this country; was infinitely beloved, being a good friend to all the peasants, and encouraging them in every thing. The 3d in the morning I set out for his house, and got there by breakfast. I was introduced to him in company of his wife, and fix or feven children of different ages; and delivering M. le Count de Roncellen's letter, he read it with feeming pleafure, and with the utmoft politenefs welcomed me to Raversburg, the name of his feat. The Count had fully explained to him the motives of my travels through Sweden, which he was pleafed to commend very much. He is a lufty man, of about fifty years of age, with a fine open manly countenance, that prejudices one at firft fight in his favour. He fpeaks French fluently; had been in England, but not long enough to learn the language. He made many enquiries after M. de Roncellen, and his improvements, while we breakfafted; faid that he had not been able of fome years to pay him a vifit, but that he hoped once more to have that pleafure, if he lived. He told me he had a packet for me, directed under my name, *An Englifh gentleman on his travels through Sweden.* This he gave me in the afternoon, and I found it a letter from Baron Miftler at Stockholm, with cafh to the amount of forty-feven pounds, the product of the fale of chaife and horfes, which I thought a very good return in Sweden. M. Verfpot asked me concerning my route; and was much furprifed at finding that I had penetrated through the whole province of Dalecarlia. He faid, it it was a bold undertaking, and tho' he had travelled through moſt parts of Sweden, yet he had ſeen very little of that province. I gave him a curſory account of what I had remarked among the peaſants there, with which he ſeemed to be pleaſed; and attended very much to what I mentioned of their husbandry. He ſaid that I had ſeen ſuch great things at the Count de Roncellen's, that every thing he could ſhew me would appear ſmall; tho' he had ſome improvements, which perhaps I might like to ſee, as I appeared to be fond of agriculture.

He then told me, that for twenty years he attended the government of Sweden as a ſenator, and was long anxious to oppoſe a party, that ſeemed determined on the ruin of their country; but finding, after a ſtruggle of many years, that the voice of prudence and moderation was ſo little liſtened to, he took a long farewel of them, and retired to this eſtate, determining to make a country life, which was before only a ceſſation from buſineſs, the only buſineſs of his life; and ſince he took that reſolution, he has adhered to it without once quitting it; and from the factions which have ariſen ſince his departure, he has had continual reaſon to rejoice at the determination. He has found in the obſcurity of theſe moun-

mountains a satisfaction which the busiest scenes of Stockholm could never give. He applied himself to the study and practice of agriculture with great eagerness, and has always taken uncommon pleasure in trying various experiments on different articles of culture, to discover the most profitable application of the ground; and he has found, that the only way for a Swedish nobleman to be rich, or to improve his income in a manner that may bring no regret with his wealth, is the improvement of his estates. Nothing is so profitable, nor any thing, in Sweden at least, so honourable. He has been much ridiculed for giving up an attention to the government of his country, to retire and pass his days among peasants and boors. " But experience has told me," added M. de Verspot, " that my choice has been right; for I have increased my wealth at the same time that I have improved the happiness of my life." This account, which he gave me in a pleasing candid manner, shewed me at once that his ideas were congenial with those of the illustrious Roncellen.

He did not carry me to his improvements that day; but after breakfast he took a walk with me, which lasted till dinner; in which I viewed the grounds around his house, the

situa-

situation of which is one of the most romantic I ever beheld. It is a very large quadrangular building around a court, situated on the side of a vast mountain, near the bottom, but not so low as not to command a great view in front: a large track of falling ground parts the house from a very beautiful lake, four miles long, and one and an half broad, in which are several lofty islands covered with wood, in one of which M. de Verspot has built a summer-house, deliciously situated: on the other sides of this lake the country is extremely various, either irregular vales, or hills rising very boldly, and in general covered thick with wood: the whole country belongs entirely to him for several miles every way: on the side of one of the hills, less steep than the rest, he has built a new village, of above seventy houses; which, being raised of a white stone, has a most chearful and enlivening appearance. In the lake he has a small ship to two masts, carrying ten brass cannon; three sloops, and various boats; all which add uncommonly to the beauty of the scene. In a word, it put me more in mind of a nobleman's ornamented seat, in a wild part of Britain, than any place I had seen since I left England. We rambled for some miles about this fine wild and romantic scene; and returning

to

to dinner, Madam de Verſpot asked me how I liked Raversburg? I replied, I thought it the moſt beautiful, and at the ſame time the moſt romantic place I had ever ſeen in my life. At which compliment, tho' indeed the mere unaffected idea I had of the place, ſhe ſeemed pleaſed; and I thought her husband very fortunate in having a lady that could reliſh theſe ſorts of country beauties, and enjoy a rural life as well as the gaieties of the capital.

M. de Verſpot lives in a very plentiful, and at the ſame time elegant ſtile.——His table is ſpread with all the delicacies which art can procure in this northern climate; he has all the fineſt wines in Europe, and his lake furniſhes him with admirable fiſh.--His eſtabliſhment may be gueſſed, when I mention his having above ſeventy menial ſervants in the houſe, one of whom has the title of captain of the guard, after the cuſtom of Sweden, who has a table, at which is his ſecretary, and two chaplains; and beſides this, there are five other tables kept; at the loweſt of which all the peaſants who pleaſe to come are indiſcriminately admitted; and their number is very often great, even to ſome hundreds; but that is only on feſtivals: however ſome take advantage of the admiſſion every day in the year. The houſe was built

by

by himself from the ground, and the situation, as I before mentioned, most judiciously chosen. The apartments are amazingly numerous, and many of them very large; I think it is the largest house belonging to a subject which I have any where seen: there is a suite of eleven rooms fronting the lake, not one of which is less than 40 feet long by 30 broad; they are all well furnished, each with two chimney-pieces in the English taste, tho' stoves are at each end of the room; and in all these stoves, and chimnies, as well as in every room of the house, are constant fires all winter. I am convinced that in such a family as this, the depth of winter would be the season to enjoy the hospitality of the owner. My only doubt is, whether they have a society collected sufficient to make that dreary season pass pleasantly.

In the morning M. de Verspot made several enquiries of me concerning various objects which I had examined in my travels in Flanders, Germany, and Denmark; when I described to him the encouragements all the useful arts had lately met with in the last of those countries: he said, that formerly the Swedes much excelled the Danes in every thing; they were equally superior in war, commerce, and agriculture; but since faction has usurped

the

the reins of the government, the kingdom of all things have much declined. I replied, that the natural advantages of Denmark were, for the fize of the territory, greater than thofe of Sweden, the climate warmer, and no mountains in the whole kingdom: but what might be cultivated to the very tops; whereas in Sweden the mountains occupy an amazing fhare of the whole kingdom, and the climate is much feverer. All that, faid he, is very true; but what is the amount of the plains of Denmark in fpace, compared to thofe of Sweden? we have twenty acres to their one; and tho' our mountains cannot be cultivated, yet they in timber, iron, copper, pitch and tar, prove as valuable as the plains; and tho' our climate is much colder than that of Denmark, yet that is of no effential confequence, as we can raife every product that is to be met with in Denmark.

I acknowledged the juftnefs of thefe remarks.

Sir, faid he, Denmark exceeds us in nothing but the encouragement given by the crown in favour of ufeful undertakings; whereas the cafe is very different in Sweden. We have had our encouragements too, but the mifchief is, they have been calculated more

for

for the advantage of the eftates of the fenators, than for that of the people at large.

Upon my making enquiries concerning the object of his rural improvements, he anfwered, I will shew you to-morrow morning a large track of cultivated country near this houfe, which, when I came to the eftate, was all wafte; my great object has been, to bring thefe waftes into improvement. My property in thefe wilds is fo extenfive, that two lives, longer than mine, would be too fhort to improve them all, but I am not idle. I keep improving—doing that land firft that lies neareft to my dwelling. I am not an enemy to woods, provided they are duly regulated, and that they are confined to land which is improper for corn and grafs. Our firs and pines thrive as well, or I think rather better, on almoft inacceffible mountains and fteeps, than on plains, and more level ground: to the former therefore I confine them; and in the management of them I am attentive always to thin my woods, inftead of deftroying the whole growth, which is the cuftom of this country. If an acre of land has thirty trees on it, that will turn out profitable to cut: the general way of the country is to cut down all, to take away the beft, and reduce the reft to afhes, for manuring the land; the

con-

consequence of which management is, the land so cleared being a long while before it is again covered with a good growth, and never with any equal to what was before upon it; this is owing to a want of shelter. While the ground is half or three fourths covered, the young trees are well sheltered, and you have a continually thriving crop. There should not be more than from five to ten trees taken out in a year from an acre of land, according as the soil, &c. may be. By practising this method, my woods yield me a very beneficial regular crop; I carry none but fine trees, which are sure of good price, to market; and am always in possession of as many acres at one time as at another, instead of having large tracks laid waste by my peasants which are some centuries before they recover themselves. Another circumstance, very well understood in England, but no where else that I have remarked, is, attending to the fences around the woods; I keep all mine in as good order as those which surround my corn : cattle love to browze in woods, but the mischief they do is incredible: upon my system, I depend for the regular supply on young trees being constantly on the growth among the old ones; but if cattle had admission in the common way, I should be presently disappointed

in

in my expectations: this is one reason why a piece of waste is so long before it becomes covered with a full growth of wood. But I make it a rule, as fast as I advance my improvements, to leave no wastes behind me. All that are not proper for corn or grass, I inclose, with the same attention as my other grounds, and sow them regularly with seeds, so that they presently become as good woods as any on my estate. For other purposes than the exportation or use of fine timber, I reserve the woods that are situated on places which would admit a profitable culture of corn or grass; these I root out entirely, as they are wanted; and, as fast as they are cleared, cultivate the land.

By means of this conduct, all the parts of my estate through which I advance my improvements, are brought into profit: woods indeed, in a country where they are so amazingly plentiful, will not pay me near so good a rent as my cultivated land; but then all they do pay is clear profit, for I leave them no where that corn and grass could be well cultivated upon.

From this conversation of M. de Verspot, I entertained great expectations of seeing many noble improvements next morning; but he warned me not to form too great an idea of them.

them.—" You will fee," faid he," good common husbandry exercifed over a large track of land; but that fight to an Englifhman is nothing; he fees it almoft over a whole kingdom. I am fo unfortunate as to be at a diftance from the fea; our river, which carries down floats of timber, is of excellent ufe; but had I the opportunity which my excellent friend Roncellen has, I would attempt to rival him. My eftate would alone furnifh employment for ten fail of ftout fhips for a century to come: had I the conveniency of a port, I fhould form a great exportation of various products, which would be an improvement which nothing elfe can equal."

M. de Verfpot ordered an early breakfaft, that we might have the longer excurfion before dinner. I was apologizing for being troublefome to him; but he faid,—" You are much miftaken, Sir, fo far from being a trouble, it is giving me the pleafure of a companion in my ufual ride, for I am never in the houfe from breakfaft to dinner."

In the morning we mounted, and he conducted me about a mile and half through the ornamented environs I mentioned before, and then came into a part of the lands which he cultivates himfelf. The fituation of the ground was in general that of fome gentle hills

hills and plains, entirely in culture. The fields were all regularly difpofed in fquares or oblongs; the fences regular and admirable; and all the gates, rails, &c. very good and neat, and all painted white, very much in the manner and appearance of many ornamented farms I have feen in England. The inclofures were in general of twenty or thirty acres. The foil is a light loam upon a rock or flint, of various depths, but feldom lefs than fix inches. M. de Verfpot obferved, that the depth was not of any material confequence, except for carrots, turneps, and fome other roots; yet thofe crops yield abundantly in only fix inches depth, tho' not fo greatly as when deeper. The fields were covered with wheat, barley, oats, peas, beans, buckwheat, carrots, turneps, clover, trefoile, &c. and many of them in natural grafs. The crops were all exceeding vigorous, and fuperior to any thing in appearance not only that I had lately feen, but alfo to moft that I recollected having taken any notice of in England. I expreffed my furprize, that this northern latitude fhould admit the crops which I then faw. " Sir, faid he, I do not wonder at your opinion; I have heard it from feveral, and read much the fame ideas in many books; nothing fo common as, in the defcription of countries, to read of the climate being fo fevere, that the inhabitants muft live only on fifhing and hunting, or produces only a few oats; twenty books in my library tell me that wheat will not fucceed higher in Sweden than the fixtieth degree of latitude. I am convinced that the bounty of Providence is fuch, that all kinds of corn, pulfe, and roots, which are now on my farm, will grow every where; the great thing is to confult the nature of the climate in the mode of culture.

In Sweden our winters are extremely fevere, and they come with but little intervention of autumn; they likewife go away fuddenly, without fuch a gradation of fpring as you have in England: fpring and autumn, you muft well know, are in warmer climates the principal feafons for moft of the operations of tillage: we are not totally without them, as fome authors affert, but their duration is very fhort. As foon as the fun has thoroughly thawed the earth, and it is in order for tillage, that is the time to fow, which is evidently evinced by the immediate vegetation feen in all plants: the peafants follow this idea very well; but the great object is the preparation of the land in the little autumn we have. The field, which they fow in fpring, never had any tillage fince the preceding crop;—fo that the products are small, not from the fault of the land, but for want of better tillage. The power of the sun coming after the frosts of winter, with the one ploughing they give their fields, sets all the weeds loose; and they vegetate with vigour, like every thing else; oftentimes to the destruction of the crop. But my method has usually been to be very expeditious; the moment harvest is over, I plough up all my stubbles before the frost catches me: by this means, when it comes, it has the greater effect; but the principal use of it is, the seeds and roots of weeds vegetating before I plough and sow in the spring, which they will not a tenth part do if the land was not stirred in autumn; by turning them in at the same time that I sow my corn, they are killed, and the crops succeed as clean as you now see them."

This conduct struck me very much, as it appeared at once to be founded not only in experience, but good sense. Upon my asking him, if he thought ploughing up of stubbles in autumn would be a good practice, where the same inducement did not hold equally strong, that is in milder climates, such as England?—"There is not, replied he, the same reason for it, because your spring allows you to plough your land as often as you please pleafe before you fow, confequently the weeds may be deftroyed: yet I fhould follow the rule even in that climate; becaufe by ploughing before winter, (for which likewife you have whatever time you want) the frofts will have much more power over the foil, in breaking and fweetening it; fo that lefs tillage would do in the fpring, and the weeds alfo grow much more, which will render it fo much the eafier to kill them."—What the practice of our Englifh farmers is in this cafe, I do not know: but it appears to be a point of confiderable importance.

As we rode through the fields, the crops of which made fo fine an appearance, M. de Verfpot obferved, that of all his grain nothing paid him better than wheat; tho' among the common farmers they are much inclined to think that oats anfwer as well, from the largenefs of the produce, which is much greater than wheat. My oat crops generally yield me five or fix quarters an acre; my barley rather more than four; wheat yields two and an half; peas as much; beans four; and buckwheat four. Thefe crops feeming to me to be very confiderable, I asked him if he did not manure very richly for them; and how he managed in this refpect, as he did not ufe woodafhes in the large quantities of the common farmers?

"I depend, replied he, entirely upon dung, formed into composts with the earth I dig in draining marshes. I have two strong reasons against the practice common among the peasants, of manuring with such quantities of wood-ashes; first, they spoil for ages large tracks of wood land, for they not only carry away all the ashes, but all the surface of the soil with them; and I find my woods too profitable to destroy, without at the same time gaining either grafs or arable in the room of them: secondly, they depend so much on these ashes, that they are apt to neglect the article of cattle, as they can manure their lands without them: but I think it an infinite loss, not only to themselves, but to the whole kingdom, to adopt any system that lessens the general stock of cattle; I think they form the most profitable part of husbandry; and at the same time that they are of this importance to the farmer, in the profit they yield, they are to the state the foundation of the manufactures of wool and leather, which in all countries are of such consequence. Nor do their benefits stop here; for our corn fields are indebted to them for the finest crops that cover them. Did the peasants depend on their dung alone for manuring, they would keep more cattle, and then their general husbandry would

would be much improved. In all my improvements, when I proportion the quantities of each crop to the reft, I make the firft foundation of fuch an arrangement, the quantity of dung I fhall want; I then provide food for fuch a number of cattle as will I know yield me the requifite quantity of dung. I have carried this idea into practice thefe many years, and always found it uniformly profitable."

Upon my enquiring further into this fyftem, he went on—" A very little attention would enable our peafants to conceive the full extent of this management, and act accordingly. They all of them keep a few cattle, and know well enough how to crop their fields for the maintenance of them, fo that they would only have to proportion their ground to a greater number. They all of them feel the advantage of keeping cows, hogs, oxen, and many of them fheep; they find nothing of a readier fale, and in many fituations they are the only commodities which, for want of roads, can be brought to market. And tho' our winter is very long, and the maintenance of them at that feafon troublefome and expenfive, yet there are few cold climates that produce better crops for keeping them ; and it is in the winter alone that the dunghills are made,

made, which are of such great value to all our crops. Our Swedish turneps, of which we have two sorts, is a most valuable crop; when prepared for by sufficient ploughings and manure, it yields a vast produce, which will keep sound through the sharpest winter: for the sake of tilling my land, and being able to get at the crop at all times, I generally lay them up in barns, so as to be very handy for feeding all sorts of cattle on the spot. We have the plants which you in England call the kales, that is, cabbages, which do not turn in with hard heads, but are all composed of open leaves; these vegetate all winter through, and the snows must be uncommonly deep, to prevent our getting at them. Carrots I lay by in stores, in the same manner as turneps: then we have plenty of hay and straw in common with other countries; so that I must confess I see no reason for our complaining in Sweden,—nor any difficulty which our industrious farmer can find in providing for the most numerous herds of cattle. An acre of turneps or carrots will winter-feed four cows, if they have a good portion of hay, and as much straw as they like; but without any hay at all they will keep three; which is very considerable, and shews what may be done by a spirited industry. Our kale grows into such fine crops,

crops, that, with ſtraw, an acre of it will winter fix ſheep; ſwine are kept in the moſt advantageous manner poſſible on carrots, and even fattened upon them to great profit. But all theſe crops, to be conſiderable, ought to be very well tilled, and amply manured; and if the peaſants are reſtrained from wood-aſhes, and have not any cattle, from whence is this manure to come? Hence it is, that cattle enable you to keep cattle—ſo that the more they keep, the more they might keep, if the dung is properly applied.

Another great advantage poſſeſſed by all wild countries, is the having great plenty of vegetables, of uſe only for being converted into litter: all our waſtes and our woods yield vaſt quantities of weeds, which, mown in their ſucculency, make excellent ſtraw for littering our cattle all winter long, which in the raiſing much manure, is an advantage of the moſt valuable kind. They are to be gained in almoſt any quantities; but our peaſants do not ſee their intereſt in this point as they ought; moſt of them lay in a few loads, but not a tenth part ſufficient to make as much dung as they might. I keep all my cattle littered up to their bellies the whole winter through; by which means, my dunghills enſure me the greateſt crops, of which the

the land is capable of yielding. So that I am confident there is no abfolute occafion for fuch quantities of wood-afhes as the Swedifh peafants fo much depend on."

From the view I had of M. de Verfpot's fields, as well as from his converfation, I was extremely clear that no man could know better than he, how to raife great crops of all forts; but I defired to know where he found a market for his products, for I found he had four thoufand acres in his own hands.

"I do not, replied he, meet with any difficulty in that point; my improvements in hufbandry, and in ornamenting the lands around my houfe, with the number of people that inhabit it, all together form a very confiderable confumption, and the reft is fold by my agents to whoever will purchafe: much is bought, to fupply the miners in the mountains; and yet more finds its way down the river by Tuna, and fo to fea, to the towns upon the coaft. If I had a port fo conveniently fituated, as to make it advifable to keep fhipping of my own, I fhould be able to gain a much higher price; but as I meet at prefent with rates that anfwer very well to me, and I have neither trouble nor chances, I am contented; but if the people on my eftate increafe in future as they have done lately, the whole

whole country will find a market at home superior to any thing they can get abroad.

And from the experience I have had in this point, I have great reason to believe that increasing population brings with it every other advantage, and that most other improvements will follow of course, provided the population so gained is founded on husbandry—that is, a certainty of food. I have never formed any manufactories, because I was of opinion that the improvement of the soil was the first and most profitable business the people could be employed in—and that 'till husbandry-improvements were advanced to the utmost height, all the hands employed in the manufactures were so much loss to the state.

This reasoning I know I am particular in; it will give offence to you, and would give yet more to a Frenchman.——But whether I am right or wrong, is not a point of any consequence, since they generally establish themselves without your assistance. The number of people I have drawn together for different works, have formed manufactories; the ready market this population carries with it, has induced several undertakers to fix some fabrics in my villages; there are some of woollen cloth, of leather, linen, hats, and hardware: they are not, it is true, considerable; but they are

are proportioned to the demand, and population has created them; and I have no doubt but they will increase as the population of my estate increases. Thus you may depend upon it in all cases, that if you work such improvements in agriculture as greatly increases the number of people, such improvements will themselves do all the rest; they will establish manufactures, and bring commerce when they arrive at a certain degree, and wealth proportioned must be the consequence. Nor should we forget, that when these kind of advantages take place of themselves, and gradually, we may be sure they are natural, and permanent, and not exotics, planted by an anxious hand, and cherished by an unremitting attention: such must be more valuable, and always more certain in their nature and consequences; and I conclude from hence that the sollicitude discovered at present in several parts of Europe, for establishing manufactories, is either unnecessary or improper: if their policy is sound, manufacture will come of course; if they do not come, it is proof sufficient that they ought not, as the hands which they would employ ought to be advancing the soil to its utmost improvement, before any thing is done in fabrics."

I made

I made some objections to this opinion, drawn from the example of England and Holland; but they were not of consequence enough to insert here.———M. de Verspot went on———" In conversing with several noblemen in Sweden, on the subject of improving their estates, the most general difficulty I have heard of is the getting hands; but from my own experience I am clear that this is an imaginary evil. No country could be more desolate, or worse inhabited than this, when I began my undertaking of improving it; but by protecting and encouraging them, building houses immediately for all that would settle, and employing them constantly at a fair price for their labour, they would any where command whatever numbers they wanted, and increase them as quickly as they pleased to any height. I am convinced, that for increasing the population of any country, nothing more is wanting than the improvement of land."

Having viewed a considerable part of the farm, we returned to dinner; and spent the remainder of the day in conversing on these subjects. I found him quite enthusiastical in favour of agriculture; but must say, that I believe he would not, if he had the direction of the affairs of Sweden, carry these ideas exclusively

sively too far, and neglect manufactures and commerce too much.

The next morning he carried me over a different part of his farm, and shewed me the improvement of a very large marsh, by draining. It was converted into a very profitable meadow. He also carried me through a field of experiments, of fifty acres, wherein he tries every thing that is of dubious success, before he extends the culture through his whole farm: here he brings the recommendations of various writers to the test, to see what truth there is in their assertions: he is now trying some artificial grasses, not yet common in Sweden, particularly sainfoine, esparcette, lucerne, and cytissus, of all which he had small parcels, but he did not seem to speak favourably of them, from what they had hitherto promised. He had also under culture several plants from Siberia, and different sorts of wheat, to see which would agree best with the climate. Here was also a set of trials upon dung, in order to discover what was the proper quantity for an acre of land. I must own that this field pleased me better than any one I had ever viewed in my life. M. de Verspot here gained most of his knowledge.—the culture of it is immediately under his own inspection—nothing is done here without he is

present;

present; and by repeating and varying his trials, he is able to decide in every inftance what beft fuits the foil and climate. He obferved to me, that no farmer fhould be without a piece of ground which he dedicates to this ufe; otherwife he muft either give up all idea of any improvements, or elfe try them upon too great a fcale at firft; which, if they are unfuccefsful, would be injurious to him: a remark which is certainly juft.—The evening of this day was alfo fpent in converfation, which I found very inftructive.

The 6th I took my leave of him, after expreffing how much I was obliged to him for my reception at Raversburg, and inviting him, in cafe he fhould ever come into England again, or any of his friends, to give me an opportunity of returning it. I had enquired of him concerning the northern provinces of Sweden; and he affured me that I fhould fee nothing in Lapland worth going after; that as my route was to Petersburg, I had better keep pretty near the coaft of the Baltic, through the two Bothnias, down to Finland, and through Nyland and Carelia; in which journey I fhould have an opportunity of feeing feveral varieties of country and husbandry.

CHAP.

CHAP. II.

Hernosand—Pleasing Adventure with a Swedish Peasant—Husbandry—Uma—State of commerce—Pitha—Description of the country—Torneo—State of the country in East Bothnia—Admirable Management of a Farmer—A Swedish Club—Remarkable Country—Nyslot—Wyburg.

I LEFT Raversburg the 6th, setting out for Hernosand on the Baltic, in the province of Angermania, the distance sixty miles, which took me two days, through a country very much like that about M. de Verspot, but very differently cultivated : spots in the vales were occupied by peasants, who all seemed to be little farmers, but they had nothing that struck me in their management. Hernosand is a small island in the gulf; it is the capital of the province, and has a little trade in iron and timber, and is a port to which some small craft come, that ply backwards and forwards from Stockholm. It might be of very great advantage, that so large a part of this kingdom is situated on the Baltic, and surrounds

the

the gulf of Bothnia in such a manner, that a quick and easy communication is kept up between province and province, and between them all and the capital. I know of scarcely any country that has the advantage of such a navigation as this gulf, which is surrounded by so many provinces.

The 8th I reached Scenfio, a little village on a bay of the gulf, the inhabitants of which support themselves chiefly by fishing; great quantities of which they dry for their winter provision; and there are some sorts which, when dried, they pull in pieces, and grind, and then make up in balls of fish bread, being mixed with a portion of barley meal. It is a very odd, and I should apprehend a very unwholsome diet. They have but little idea of husbandry here; which would make one think that it is in general carried on in the villages merely as a means of existence, by raising food, and seldom as a trade wherewith to get money, in order to purchase necessaries. The peasants in every part of Sweden go to market for fewer commodities than we in England can have any conception of. Their husbandry, hunting or fishing feeds them; most of their cloathing is of their own manufacture; many of them wear wooden shoes of their own making; so that salt and
Vol. III.			D			some

some brandy are the chief articles that many of them purchase.—This was a journey of near forty miles.—The 9th I went near as far to get to Grunsud: the country is chiefly peopled with fishermen, but they have more culture among them than in that of yesterday's route. Many of them have little farms, and seem to be much more at their ease than those that are mere fishermen. From this place to Una in West Bothnia, at the distance of seventy miles, took me a day and a half; the country is pretty well cultivated. I lodged at the house of a peasant, who had a small farm of his own, and is, I believe, the most contented, happy man in the world. I offered him money; but he would take none, saying, that when he travelled through my country, he dared to say I should not refuse him a night's lodging, and some victuals.—The honest man did it from a mere principle of genuine hospitality. Money, said he, is of very little value to me; my farm supplies myself and my family with most necessaries; and plenty to sell for the little we want to buy. He had a wife, two sons, and two daughters; and the whole family seemed animated with the father's spirit.—There was a chearfulness, a health, and an activity in them all that convinced me they were superlatively happy. The employment of the

three

three men was to hunt, shoot, and fish, and do the most laborious works of the husbandry; the women ploughed and sowed the ground, and did most of the other business of the farm that was within their strength, and manufactured woollen cloth for all the family. The sale of their superfluities bought them whatever they wanted to purchase, such as salt, implements, some linen, &c. and they had money enough always left, after paying their taxes, to lay up something against emergencies. I think this is as compleat a representation of rural happiness as can exist.— This family has nothing to fear.—They are as independent as an absolute monarch, and much more at their ease. It was with pleasure I entered into the particulars of their living, and found a cottage that was the constant residence of peace and content. It is in such situations and circumstances that we should look for happiness; not in towns, the palaces of kings, or the seats of gentlemen, but in the humble cottage, where no knowledge enters but what is applied to utility.

Una, where I arrived the 21st, is one of the most considerable towns in West Bothnia. It is situated on a very fine large river, which falls into the gulf: there is a good harbour for
ships,

ships, and the place has a pretty brisk trade in timber, iron, pitch, tar, &c. And having two or three merchants, of large property, to whom several ships belong, they carry on here a trade with Holland and England, loading out with the products of the countries around the gulf, and bringing home a great variety of commodities, which they sell in all the ports around the Baltic, in Sweden, Russia, Livonia, Poland, Prussia and Germany. It is of very great advantage to a town to be inhabited by a few such extensive traders; for the profits center in it; they employ their townsmen in their shipping, and export much more products than would be done if it were not for them. These merchants also much enrich the place by their ship-building; for they have never less than three or four on the stocks at a time: these ships they sell wherever they can get a market, cargo and all, which they often do to good advantage; and this I take to be the most beneficial commerce which Sweden, or any other country that abounds with plenty of naval stores, can carry on; for by building ships for sale, she gives the last hand in manufacturing all her products, and consequently employs as many of her people as possible; but when she sells the timber, iron, pitch, &c. separately, the nations that buy them make
this

this laſt profit, which is a very conſiderable one. No government, therefore, can ever give a wiſer bounty than that of ſo much per ton for all ſhips built in a country; it is the moſt advantageous commerce her ſubjects can carry on. Louis XIV. was certainly well adviſed by Colbert to give this bounty; and it was attended with as good effects as any other meaſure in that ſuccefsful adminiſtration.

It took me two days to reach Scornfay, at the diſtance of fourſcore miles. I took up my quarters the firſt night at a village, where, for the firſt time ſince I have been in Sweden, I met with a ſet of barbarians: I could perſuade none of them to let me into their cottages; they were ſure I was a ſpy from the Muſcovites; on what errand, or for what purpoſes I was come, they could not tell. We were now benighted, and in a road of which we had no good accounts; ſo I found I was very likely to paſs the night on horſeback: I went from cottage to cottage, but all were poſſeſſed of the ſame idea,—none would be hoſpitable. Going yet further, I came to a cottage in a lonely ſpot; I determined here to force an entrance, and ſeize the caſtle by ſtorm, in caſe they would not be prevailed on by fair and mild requiſitions: but ſtill it was in vain; they

they had no room for us: tho' we offered to pay for every thing we should eat and drink, and for our horses, yet it had no effect. I gave a signal (which I had explained to my men) for one of them to march round, and attack the fortress in flank, while I remained to storm it in front. The plan was executed in a moment: I drew my pistols, presented them to the breast of the peasant; my men bound him hand and foot; and we secured the women and children, tying all their hands behind them, and locking them up in a room, with the postilion armed as a sentinel over them: then we took possession of the mansion, feasted on the coarse provisions we found, and I set up my bed in one of the rooms. I passed a good night, without any alarm from the prisoners. In the morning I set forward on my journey, leaving the inhospitable owners of the cottage bound, till their neighbours, close to their door, and in sight of the road, should accidentally come to their relief.

Scornfay is a little town, at the foot of a mountain, with a river running under its walls near as large as the Thames at Chelsea; the shores are very bold, and all covered with wood. I have scarcely seen a more romantic and striking situation: large ships come up to the quay, tho' at a considerable distance

from

from the fea; thefe load timber chiefly, and in general for the Holland market. There are not any merchants of fubftance in the town, and their trade does not feem to be at all regular; fometimes they have three or four veffels in port, and they informed me, that, many weeks, none at all were to be feen.

From Scornfay, two days journey carried me to Tame, through a country various; but about the villages there is in general fome cultivated land, enough to feed and maintain the inhabitants, and to enable them to buy of the fhipping what they wanted, which their own foil could not furnifh. There are no fhops or pedlars upon this coaft, except in the more confiderable towns: all the peafants and inhabitants buy what they want out of fmall floop traders, which make annual voyages up the gulf of Bothnia from Stockholm. This place is in 65 degrees of latitude; and yet I perceived no change in the climate, or in the hufbandry. They cultivate the fame plants as are to be feen to the fouthward, and apparently with the fame fuccefs. Probably the increafed length of day, proportioned to the degree of north latitude, enables them to cultivate the crops of the fouthern latitudes. Barley is a tender grain, and more congenial to the climate of

Spain

Spain than any other; yet they have good crops of barley here; and I am assured they also sow it with success in Lapland; so that these most useful plants are by Providence sent to almost all countries.

The 26th I got to Pitha, the distance near thirty miles, through a country in general of a marshy soil, which some of the peasants have converted, by draining out spots into profitable meadows; and indeed I have seen in few places more industry than is apparent in these people. Upon the drier rising grounds they have crops of turneps and kale for their own and their cattle's winter provision, the meadows affording them nothing at that season. They keep large herds of swine, and feed them in winter on regular trusses of boiled roots, mixed with small quantities of peas; and they seem to reckon their hogs among the principal articles of their wealth.

Pitha is a pleasant little sea port, tolerably well built; at which they carry on a small coasting trade, and export some timber, &c. I met with a better inn here than I had done for a long while before, and a very civil, intelligent landlord. He gave me for my supper an excellent dish of fish, and a piece of very tender good venison, with some French wine, than which I had drank worse. All this made
deli-

delicate fare, compared with what I met with at the peasant's; and my reckoning was very reasonable. I asked the landlord some questions about the present state of the town, and the neighbouring country. He said it was a poor town, and a still poorer country; that if it was not for a little shipping now and then, they would have no such thing as money among them. He said trade declined, and there was no prospect of seeing things better. He entered into a long dissertation upon the politics of the times, and was deep read, I found, in the Stockholm gazette.

My next day's journey, the 27th, was to Lula, another sea port town, standing on the mouth of a very fine river, which is navigable a good way, and comes far, from the inner parts of Lapland, &c. Here is a brisker coast trade carried on than at Pitha, because the inland navigation is much more considerable. They have ships very often from Stockholm, which bring various commodities in exchange for the products of these provinces, which consist of timber, pitch and tar, and many furs; which find a good market in the capital. They are sometimes visited by English and Dutch ships, which they reckon highly advantageous to them; and from the appearance of their stocks of timber, I should think

them

them very well provided for loading any ships whatever. They have one or two pretty confiderable merchants among them, who build ships here, then load them with timber, and next fend ship and cargo to be fold in Holland upon commiffion. The profits of this, they faid, are not great; but when their feamen are out of employment, and they have the opportunity of building cheap, it pays them fomething for their trouble and rifque.

The 28th I fet out for Torneo, through a country very wild and mountainous, with but few villages in it; and as to a gentleman's feat, I had not feen one for feveral days. They have fome appearance of cultivation around their cottages; but it is only for their own fubfiftence: there is enough, however, to fhew that, high as the latitude of this country is, (it is about 66°) it would produce plentifully for a numerous people; but it is very thinly inhabited. Through all the provinces of Sweden that I have yet travelled, I am convinced that the principal caufe of the country being fo thinly inhabited, is the fmall number of farmers; there being only peafants, with land enough round their cottages, for the fubfiftence of the people within them. Many of thefe little fpots belong

belong to them; and none of the children of one will ever brook the living in a worfe manner than their fathers did, which feems to be a prevalent idea amongft them: fo that a family in this fituation are fure to leave but one reprefentative, unlefs fome gentleman builds cottages, and gives away his land around them, which it may eafily be imagined is not very common. This prevents marriages among the fons; for, as they cannot have their own cottages and lands, they live at home unmarried, with the brother who inherits: thus little or no increafe happens, unlefs by mere accident. But if all thefe peafants lived in hired cottages, without any land, and the country was cultivated by great farmers, who could afford to pay them money for their labour, the farmers would grow ten times the produce which is now produced, and export all that was not confumed; which would be a conftant motive to them to increafe their bufinefs, and of courfe to fix their fons in other farms. In the cafes of fome patriotic perfons, who have made improvements in husbandry, and built houfes, we found, before, that the people increafed as faft as could be wifhed.

Torneo ftands better than any other town on the gulf, for the trade of Lapland, which

is

is not inconfiderable in furs, fome of which are very valuable. It lies near three confiderable rivers, which flow through all Swedifh Lapland, and opens a fmall commerce with Norway and Mufcovite Lapland; fo that at Torneo I found more fhipping than I had feen at any place I had lately been at on this fea. Ships come from Stockholm hither, laden with all forts of neceffaries for thefe northern provinces, and carry their products back in return. Hence the town is tolerably well built, the ftreets broad and ftraight, and very well paved, and fome of the merchants, of which there are a good number, very rich. They build fhips, and fit them out on trading voyages, and make every effort to employ their money fo as it may bring in good intereft; but, with all their endeavours, they are not able to increafe the trade of the place, further than what the fame men would carry on at any other; which is owing to a want of population, and wealth in the country behind them; fo that they are much limited in the commodities they export, and alfo in the quantity of thofe they import. And indeed it is generally found that agriculture, well purfued, muft increafe the people very much; manufactures will next arife, to fatisfy their greateft wants; and then comes commerce,

to

to supply the rest. This is the natural chain, and it is in vain to think of breaking or reversing it.

July 31st I left Torneo, and reached Coyrannum, a little town on the coast, which is subsisted chiefly by fishing. The inhabitants in the most northerly parts of the two Bothnia's have a different appearance from the Swedes in the southern provinces of the kingdom; they are less informed, of a shorter stature, and more irregular in their dress, many of them sewing together the skins of foxes, and other wild creatures, whose furs are not of value, and make their cloathing in a much rougher and more ordinary manner; nor are they so intelligent or comprehensive; but they are a very simple and harmless people, and appear to be very humane. I found most of them exceedingly respectful and civil. Their ordinary saluation is not bowing, like the Swedes in other parts: these countrymen take hold of your right-hand, and lay it over their left, making strange faces at the same time. The next town, of the least consequence, is Salo, which carries on a very small trade, they informed me; the distance is near eighty miles, which I performed in two days. And here let me say a word or two in praise of the little Dalecarnian horses, which

which have brought me with such expedition through some of the most dangerous roads in Europe, and without having once failed us, tho' six in number; and I think they look as well, as before they set out on a journey of so many hundred miles. I have so great a value for them, that I am determined to carry them to England; and I am now so accustomed to the hard exercise of riding thirty or forty miles a day, that I feel not the least inconvenience from it.

August the 2d I got to Salo; the country through which I travelled not mountainous, being in general a plain, rising into small hills; much of it well cultivated; and, what surprized me, by farmers who hire of the landlords considerable tracks of land: their chief riches are cattle; they have large droves of black cattle, many sheep, and numerous herds of hogs. The method in which these farmers pay their labourers, the peasants, is in kind: those who attend the sheep have so many kept for them with the farmer's; the hogs the same; and the men who take care of the cattle have some cows kept for them. The landlords rent is paid in corn and cattle. All this is necessary, in a country where money is amazingly scarce. They sow wheat, and all the other sorts of grain, pulse and

roots,

roots, which I have feen in other parts of Sweden; tho' I do not think their crops are fo good as in mountainous tracks; which I apprehend is for want of equal fhelter, and the foil not being fo good as in fmall vales, that receive the wafh of many mountains. The turnep and carrot crops, with fields of kale, they cultivate, I was informed, more to the north than any place where I have been; which fhews how valuable thefe plants are for fupporting themfelves and their cattle. There are fome fhip loads of different forts of provifions that go every fummer from Salo, for Stockholm and the fouthern parts of the Baltic; they do not get money in return, but fuch manufactures and commodities as they want.

My next route was to Nicarlby, a little fea port town, with fome trifling commerce, near ninety miles from Salo. I did not get there till the 5th, twice taking up my lodging with very hofpitable farmers. One of them, at a little village called Koninglens, was much fuperior in his ideas, and in his husbandry, to any thing I had feen of late; and this was a pleafing circumftance to me, as I got to his houfe early in the afternoon. I took a walk with him through the fields nearest to his dwelling; and the accounts he gave me appeared

peared very rational. His crops were all very fine and clean; and I obferved that his corn fields were very numerous, and of large extent, fpreading over feveral hills within fight; the fize of his farm exceeding in the whole a thoufand acres, and a great portion of it under culture. He gets two quarters of wheat an acre, and fometimes more, three quarters of barley and beans, and fometimes four of oats; and his root crops all appeared very good. He told me there were feveral other farms in the neighbourhood, and that all of them belonged to the baron Bothmer, who refided conftantly at Stockholm; that money was fo fcarce in this country, that the other tenants paid the agent in kind for rent; but he finding that this was a great lofs to them, from the low prices at which the products were reckoned, thought of paying in money; and this he planned, from having once ufed the fea. All the products of their farms were at double the price, at Stockholm, to what the landlords agents allowed for them. This induced him to buy a floop of fifty tons, and to hire a couple of failors, to try a voyage to Stockholm in September, carrying a loading of wheat, barley, pork, beef, mutton, wool, furs, &c. and made it up with timber. The experiment turned out as he could wifh: he

kept

kept his sloop, persuaded one of the sailors to live with him on shore as well as aboard, and made an annual trip upon the same business for several years, paying his rent in money. He found this scheme so very advantageous that, as his husbandry increased, by improving the bad and waste lands of his farm, he found he could load his vessel twice with the marketable produce of his farm, besides what he disposed of in the neighbourhood; and he has now increased it to three voyages, which he makes regularly every year, and he himself sells the cargo. He has built a kind of shed over a dry dock, where he lays up his sloop, and is very careful of her. She will not hold out many years longer; however he proposes buying one of 80 or 100 tons, finding the method he pursues of so much consequence to his profit; for this ready sale of his products enables him every year to make improvements. He has, since he acted thus, improved a piece of the waste belonging to his farm every year; which he will continue to do, until all is in culture. I should observe, that his farm lies remarkably well for executing this work; for it is all on the sea coast; and there is a small creek runs up into a pent near his house, which has depth of water sufficient for a ship of two hun-

Vol. III. E dred

dred tons; but at the same time that he enjoys this advantage, there are hundreds of other farms, equally well situated, around the gulf of Bothnia, whereof the farmers have no notion of making such an use.

I must remark, that this instance is a proof, among many others of a different nature, of the great consequence of a regular market for the farmer in all countries to depend upon. This active and enterprizing man struck out so original a way of disposing of his products, merely for want of a market at home: had he been possessed of that, he certainly would not have been at the expence of finding one at so great a distance. Thus improvements in husbandry are not at their highest value, nor indeed can be undertaken in their due extent, without a market for the products so raised being gained. There are many ways of obtaining it: the increase of population, caused by the improvements, takes some; manufactures, to the full amount of the people's wants, provide more mouths, which carry off another large portion; and then commerce must be brought in, to carry off the remainder; first, by the number of people she fixes on the spot; and secondly, by exportation: then the having gained a full market for all that can be produced, is such an encouragement to the class who cultivates the soil, that they will necessarily carry their improvements very far: Not so far however as they are capable of going, without being pushed on by encouragement and example from those above them. Of this truth see instances every day, in the countries best peopled, and in general best cultivated, and where all the products of the lands sell at as high prices as any where else. Thus in England, what considerable tracks of land are at this day as wild as if they were in the latitude of Lapland, and amounting, according to the accounts of many knowing persons, to a seventh part of the kingdom? With us no encouragements, no markets are wanting. What therefore should be the reason of such a strange neglect? It can be owing to nothing but the ignorance and obstinacy of our lower sort of people, who will not be persuaded that any land can be good for use that was not cultivated by their forefathers; and this supineness we find amongst men who shew themselves so well qualified in the management of land already in culture. Therefore, as none of these motives are strong enough for bringing into cultivation the waste lands of any country, it is absolutely necessary that public laws and private endeavours be made to co-operate; which cannot be done, without making it the interest of landlords to undertake and encourage improvements, beyond that standing interest which the profit of the work always carries with it: for instance, it might be advisable to lay heavy taxes upon waste lands, as long as they continued uncultivated; and in case any old customs or rights, such as that of commonage upon them, should obstruct such beneficial laws, then to abolish all such antient customs, and allow every man to inclose, and do what he thought best with every part of his own property. There are many other means which might be put in execution, in order to push on all men to a vigorous resolution to improve the wastes belonging to them; and if the subject was considered with any degree of attention, numerous methods might be found for effectually answering the purpose.

It is very surprising that I should not, in travelling so many miles upon the sea coasts of Sweden, have met with more instances of this penetration than the single one of the farmer in question. This kingdom has a vast line of coast, numerous bays, gulfs that jet far into the provinces, with very many navigable rivers; and at the same time that these opportunities are so abundant, a vast track of country lies adjacent to them, in the highest want of them, and to which they would be of such use as to advance the value of the lands very confiderably. Surely this should be a very great motive to all the landlords upon these coasts, who reside upon their estates, to put in practice means so much at their command, of advancing the value of them.

Nicarlby is a place of no great confideration. They told me, it was once a town that carried on a great trade; but when the Ruffians over-run the province, they burnt it to the ground, and quite ruined several of the greatest merchants in it; since which it has never recovered its trade, the commerce at present carried on here not being at all confiderable. It is not however badly built, and the streets are regular. The church is small, but very neat. They have a trifling manufacture of very coarse woollen goods, for the supply of the neighbouring country; but it does not seem to be in a flourishing situation.

The 6th I got to Vero, another little town on the gulf, with an exceeding good port, and a tolerably built quay, which is the only good street in the town. There is a little trade upon the coast, and to Stockholm, which confifts principally of timber. There are not
above

above seven or eight hundred souls in the place, and it appears to be but a poor one. Waſſay, which I reached the 7th, is a place of greater note; it has more trade; and several merchants, tolerably wealthy, inhabit it, who have ships of their own, in which they export large quantities of timber; but they want a home demand, to load their veſſels back again; for the country behind the town, after a few miles, is one continued foreſt, without any cultivated ſpots or villages, and reaches from hence quite to the white ſea, through ſeveral Ruſſian provinces, at the diſtance of near ſeven hundred miles, and ſcarcely any inhabitants to be found the whole way. I came accidentally by this knowledge; for, juſt after I had ordered ſupper, the landlord of the inn came in to inform me, that in the next room were a ſet of gentlemen of the town, aſſembled at a club, who, underſtanding there was a ſtranger in the houſe ſent their compliments to him, inviting him to ſpend the evening with them. I thought I might as well make myſelf acquainted with a Swediſh club, and therefore returned for anſwer, that I ſhould be very happy in waiting on them; but it was my misfortune not to underſtand Swediſh, and I

had

had no interpreter but my servant. They replied, that if I underſtood French, they had one among them who could converſe with me; if not, defired I would bring my interpreter. This was very well; ſo I went to them, and, upon my entering the room, they all aroſe, and received me after the manner of the country. There were nine of them; one, who ſeemed to be the principal man amongſt them, and who was the gentleman that underſtood the French language, was a very corpulent man, who complained of being much afflicted with the gout. I found he was a merchant in the town, who had formerly been captain of a merchant ſhip; and I obſerved that they gave him the title of Captain, by way of honour; tho' I ſhould have thought it, for a man of property, rather a reflection. He was about fifty years old, a lively, talkative fellow, had travelled almoſt every part of the world; and as ſuch extenſive travelling, tho' aboard a merchant ſhip, is very uncommon, in the remote provinces of Sweden, I perceived they confidered him almoſt as an oracle, and gave way to his opinion in moſt points. He craved my name, my country, and my buſineſs in Sweden, tho' in a good-natured way. Upon my ſatisfying him in all theſe particulars, and his informing

his

his friends of it, I found I gained much in all their good graces, by thinking their country worth viewing thro' curiofity. The reſt of the company appeared to be merchants, captains of ſhips, and the better ſort of ſhopkeepers, but all decently and neatly dreſſed, and ſeemed, from the manner in which things were conducted, to be people of ſubſtance. The worſt of their company was their pipes; they all ſmoaked tobacco inceſſantly; and as the room was but a ſmall one, I thought I ſhould have been ſuffocated at firſt. They made many inquiries after England, and our manners and cuſtoms in many particulars; in which I ſatisfied them, much to their apparent entertainment. I, in my turn, queſtioned them about the manufactures and commerce of their town and neighbourhood, and they gave me an account of every thing they could, and I believe a very juſt one. They ſaid the trade of their town was at a very low ebb; that it was too inconſiderable a place, and the country around it too thinly inhabited, to furniſh much trade; but that they traded a good deal all around the Baltic, being ſatisfied with commerce whereever they found it; that they generally loaded timber for England or Holland, and then got a freight to where-ever they could; if not

on

on the merchants account, to whom they fent the timber, yet on their own, by taking in a cargo of fuch goods as they could get off at fome port or other in the Baltic, and never lofing any opportunity to fell fhip and all. This commerce, on an average of feven years, pays, they affured me, very poor intereft for their money: now and then they meet with lucky voyages, that anfwer greatly; but fometimes they are forced to go from port to port, in England and Holland, before they can fell a cargo, and perhaps at laft, after a great lofs of time, under prime coft and charges; fo that they fhould not make fuch ventures, were it not that all their trade depends upon keeping fome fhipping in motion, by forcing things in this manner. The moft profitable part of thefe voyages is the fale of the fhip, when it happens, and that they endeavour to pufh as much as pofiible, tho' at low prices, in order to keep their fhip carpenters together, by finding them conftant work. One of them faid, " Ah! Sir, we muft be very induftrious, through a long life, before we can make a fmall fortune:" which indeed, from the defcription of their trade, I thought true enough.

Upon my enquiring after their manufactures, they faid they had none, except a fabric

bric or two of very coarse woollens, for the peasants wear; and that was carried on merely because of imported goods of that sort being prohibited, tho' they could buy them in England and sell them at Wassay much cheaper than their own manufacturers could make them. But, said they, trade is shackled and destroyed by the regulations, prohibitions and laws lately made; so that if our governors go on much longer as they have done of late, we shall have no trade at all,—not a ship to navigate. We could get cargoes of many sorts of goods in England, that would go off well in Sweden, but we are prohibited; and for no good reason; for we should not pay for them with money; we could get all with timber, iron, pitch, tar, and hemp.—This would keep our ships employed; whereas your countrymen, finding that we do not take your goods, go to the Danes and the Muscovites. And for that matter who can blame you? The fault is all in our government.

I could not help smiling at the warmth of the honest merchant who said this; and, from what I have at various times heard, since I left Stockholm, I must confess I do not see the policy of the laws in relation to trade, which have been lately made in Sweden. The merchants complaining is a rule, very

rarely

rarely a falſe one, to judge by. It may be ſaid, that theſe traders and captains viſibly concern themſelves with nothing more than getting freights for their ſhips, and would like any trade, however detrimental to the kingdom, provided it anſwered their purpoſes. But in reply to this, it might be obſerved, that the ſtate of the caſe in queſtion ſtrikes out all ſuch ſuppoſitions ;—for they wanted to trade to a country, againſt whom the balance always was, in every period of the mutual commerce; conſequently a ſafe and an advantageous trade, upon the very appearance of it. They alſo wanted to load their ſhips out, as well as home, being equally deſirous of carrying out their own products, as bringing home our manufactures. At the ſame time that theſe unfavourable circumſtances appear, the navigation of Sweden is enlarged, and the moſt valuable part of all her manufactures, ſhip-building, extended: ſo that her eagerneſs to make her ſubjects manufacture every thing for themſelves, was aiming at an impoſſibility, and being, in all the intermediate ſteps, much too precipitate.

Upon my enquiring into the ſtate of the country to the eaſt of Waſſay, they told me it was one unbounded and almoſt uninhabited foreſt; that no cultivation was to be met with,

with, till I came to the province of Savolaxia, and that nine villages out of ten in that country were deſtroyed by the Ruſſians, and the people carried off, and ſettled in waſte tracks in Ingria and Carelia, where they were ſo well treated afterwards, having good lands given to every family, houſes built for them, and furniſhed; cattle given them and implements to cultivate the ground with, and at the ſame time no taxes taken of them; that they found themſelves happier under the Ruſſian deſpotiſm than under their own free government; and, as a proof of this, they have drawn away whole villages from our provinces. Upon my enquiring if it was owing to any evils attending the climate or ſoil, or its products, that ſuch a vaſt country was in ſo wild a ſtate; they replied, that, on the contrary, it was a country which would ſupport very numerous inhabitants; for the ſoil in the vales, and upon the gentle hills, was ſuppoſed to be equal to any in Sweden; and that they had lands, much more to the north, in a ſtate of profitable culture; that the foreſts are full of very fine timber, which would aſſiſt the inhabitants conſiderably in all their undertakings: In a word, that much of it was a very deſirable country, and wanted little beſides people to inhabit it.

This

This inftance of fo large a track of country being uninhabited, and the emigrations to Ruffia, I muft own, made a ftronger impreffion on me in disfavour of the prefent government, than all the circumftances I had heard before ; for I take it to be, of all others, the ftrongeft proof in the world, that there is an effential mifchief preying in the vitals of a country, when its inhabitants leave it, to fettle in the lands of other potentates. Men, who are brought up to the arts, to commerce, and are the inhabitants of towns, often emigrate, without a country being in any refpect on the decline, and even without its being a fign of any evil in the government ; becaufe there are always unquiet fpirits, and broken fortunes, in thofe claffes, that will ever be rambling : but for the peafants to find their lot fo hard, as to quit the country of their fathers, from a profpect of meeting with a better fate in another, and even in an enemy's country, is perhaps, of all other proofs that could be brought, the ftrongeft, to fhew that a government is very bad, or very badly adminiftred.

One in the company upon feeing me follicitous in thefe enquiries after thefe tracks of wafte country, faid, " If you are a gentleman of curiofity in thefe things, you may
con-

convince yourself of it: I have a small estate on the north point of the Holla lake, where are a family or two I have settled on it; I now and then take an excursion thither, for the amusement of shooting and fishing; if you will accompany me thither, I will attend you, and perhaps I may shew some sporting you will like.—I thanked him for this offer, which pleased me, on the first mention of it, but told him that I feared I should be troublesome to him in it, and that if he did not undertake the journey soon, it would not be in my power to accept the kind offer, because I was under a necessity of travelling some hundreds of leagues before winter. My good-natured Swede answered, that my company, so far from being a trouble, would be a pleasure to him, and that he would set out as soon as I pleased, as the time was perfectly equal to him; that his friend Mr. Schronburn (in the company) was to go with him, and he believed setting out soon would suit him too; which being assented to, the 9th in the morning was fixed for our departure. Upon my saying that I was bound for Petersburg, they informed me that I might have the choice of two roads; either across Swedish Finland to Abo, if I wanted to see that province, and then to coast the gulf of Finland to Petersburg;

terſburg; or elſe that I might ſtrike down
ſouth-eaſt to Wyburg, and ſo to Peterſburg,
which would be a very ſhort cut.—This I
ſaid I would conſider of. I asked Mr. Hir‐
zel (for that was the name of the merchant
who made me the offer) how many miles it
was to his eſtate? He ſaid, about one hun‐
dred and twenty, which would be near three
days journey, if I was well mounted. He
ſaid there was a cottage, about forty miles
from Waſſay, where we could lodge the firſt
night; but that the ſecond muſt be ſpent on
our horſes, for there were no more houſes.—
This is no great inconvenience, in a climate
that has ſuch long days.

This point being ſettled, we proceeded in
our converſation, and ſupper relieved me for
a time from the effluvia of their pipes. They
had ordered the beſt entertainment the town
could afford: the fiſh was the principal, and
the beſt part; there was alſo wild fowl and
veniſon. The wines were tolerable, ſome
from Spain, but chiefly Rheniſh; however,
there were three or four in the company that
ſeemed to pay their addreſſes to a bottle of
brandy, more than to any other liquor; for
they had drank it ſeveral turns, as if it was
a common beverage. All the people in theſe
northern kingdoms are immoderately fond of
ſpi‐

spirituous liquors: the severity of a long winter leads them into it so much, that they do not easily leave it off in the summer, and the excess to which they carry it is very prejudicial to their health. After supper they all took to their pipes again, to my no small mortification; and pushing the bottle about pretty briskly, they were not long altogether so clear-headed as I could have wished for, in order to have gained some more intelligence.

As it was settled that I should be in town all the next day, the principal among them, the captain, invited me to dine with him, and at the same time asked as many of the company as their avocations would allow. I accepted his invitation, and went accordingly, and found a company of six or seven; among whom was a clergyman, an elderly man, of an agreeable aspect; as he did not understand French, I was some time with but little conversation with him; but he asking me if I spoke Latin, I was taken by surprize, and after a little confusion, recollected myself enough to carry on a tolerable conversation with him afterwards, and found him a sensible, modest man. I asked him his opinion of the present state of Sweden, mentioning what had been told me the night before. He said, the account was a very true one, as to

all

all this country: I replied, laws that were general muſt generally affect the whole kingdom, and be equal every where; he ſaid no; that there were great exceptions in many inſtances in favour of the nobility, and their lands. Upon my mentioning the ſubſtance of ſome converſations I had had with a nobleman of Stockholm (meaning Baron Miſtler), he ſaid that it was partly true, but moſtly in reference to the nobility; and aſſured me that in ſeveral inſtances Sweden was in a very indifferent condition.

Part of this (as I juſt now remarked) is, I believe, true; and, as I have elſewhere obſerved, there is alſo great appearance of general good in the regulations and laws lately made for the encouragement of uſeful undertakings; and, what is of yet more conſequence, the appearance of the peaſants, &c. and the eaſy manner in which they live, and through moſt of the provinces on the other ſide the gulf of Bothnia, is a ſtrong preſumption that there is no great degree of oppreſſion among them. Therefore, the bad ſtate of affairs in the eaſtern provinces, muſt be owing in ſome meaſure at leaſt to ſome local cauſes, that have not a general effect. In this I was the more confirmed from mentioning the very bad appearance the emigration of the peaſants in the provinces adjoining the Ruffians made, which looked like a very tyrannical government; that, he faid, was not fo ftrong an inftance as it might feem; for he believed they did not fo much fly from oppreffion or want at home, as to temptation abroad; for the Ruffians had emiffaries conftantly among them, promifing mountains of rewards to all thofe that would fettle in Ruffia; and as they fully performed every thing to many of the firft emigrants, it induced numbers to follow their example; and I muft allow that the encouragement given by the Ruffians was fo much greater than it was poffible they fhould well receive in their own country, without having every thing in it reverfed; that they were really bribed away, in hopes that the fame of their treatment would occafion a continual increafe in their numbers, which has certainly taken place; though the emigrants, I am informed, do not receive the fame encouragement as formerly. Therefore, in this inftance, the depopulations of our provinces is not to be attributed to any active evil at home, but to the artful fuggeftions of a very cunning neighbour.—I replied, that it was very bad politics in the government to allow of fuch emigrations; that they fhould have ftopped them by force, if a fimple law would not have had

the

the effect.—He agreed in this, but said that if the emigrating peasants lived not upon the estates of the nobility, they cared very little about their staying in Sweden, or going to Russia: the worthy clergyman further observed, that there was not in these frontier provinces one pastor to ten flocks; so that the people had never an opportunity of being informed in any respect of what they owed to their native country.

My friend the Captain, who had made the entertainment, observed that all this was very true; but that the origin of their evils was suffering the Muscovites to conquer the Provinces around the gulf of Finland; for that brought them a neighbour that could not but prove destructive in every respect. When that nation was shut out from the Baltick, Sweden possessed most of the export trade which she now enjoys on that sea; and he justly observed that this was owing altogether to the mischiefs brought on his country by that madman Charles XII. This was a proposition that nobody could contradict; for the truth of it was evident: but I remarked that Sweden had enough left to carry her to a much higher pitch of wealth and prosperity than she at present enjoyed; her business therefore was not to regret what could not be recalled, but to do whatever her prefent fituation demanded to make amends for paft failures. They all feemed much more to wifh than to expect this.

The next morning I fet out for Mr. Hirzel's territory, having infifted upon providing my baggage, horfes, &c. the neceffary provifions for the whole journey, which I thought was the leaft I could do in return for their civility. Both Mr. Hirzel and Mr. Schornbrun were mounted on little horfes like mine, which they here call North-country horfes. For a few miles from Waffay, the country is partly cultivated; that is, you here and there fee a village, with fome cultivated lands about it; but they are thinly fcattered: and we prefently got into the wilds, wherein is no appearance of any inhabitants; and this continued through the whole day's journey of forty miles, till we came to a miferable cottage, which is a kind of ftragler from a neighbouring village, which is half depopulated. The country is chiefly compofed of one continued foreft, the trees of which are of a very fine and beautiful growth. I was curious to take notice of the appearance which the land carries in the tracks where it is clear of timber, and found that it is in general covered with a tolerable grafs; and the foil is a good rich coloured loam, tending to a clay; but in fome parts ftoney; evidently much fuperior to that of

many

many places in Sweden which are moft profitably cultivated. It was therefore extremely plain, that it was not a fault in the country, which has been the occafion of its defolate ftate.

The few inclofures around the cottage were a proof alfo of this; for although the peafant did not feem to be one of the moft induftrious; yet he had very good crops of barley and oats, and alfo of turneps, and he had a herd of cows which fed upon the wafte, with a parcel of young cattle, none of which feemed in their looks to complain of their pafture.

I fet my bed up in the fame room in which my fellow-travellers made theirs, of clean ftraw, upon which they feemed to repofe as well as on any down; which was not the worfe for an hearty fupper we had made on fifh and ham; and they paid their refpects pretty moderately to the brandy and the wine I had brought, which, with a continual fmoaking, feemed to pafs away the evening much to their fatisfaction. The next morning we continued our journey, through a wild country, which I fhould apprehend muft have been once tolerably inhabited; for we had a great road all the way, though overgrown with grafs and weeds, but faw not the leaft appearance of any habitation. The timber in this region

region is very fine, and in vaft quantities, and the foil in moft places rich and deep: it is impoffible but a good government actively exerted, might people fuch tracks of country, fo very defirable, compared with many others, well ftocked with inhabitants. We rode about thirty miles; and then, alighting, turned our horfes to graze; and, fpreading our cloth and provifions on a dry green bank, well fheltered with wood, by the fide of a ftream, we made an hearty meal, and refted ourfelves about four hours, all of us getting a nap for refrefhment: we then fet forward at an eafy pace; and, travelling through the twilight, we reached the banks of the great lake, on which my friend's plantation is, about two o'clock at noon of the 11th.

The country here is very fine. The lake is a noble one, of a varying breadth, from three to more than twenty miles over; and the length is above an hundred; there are numerous iflands in it, fome of them two or three miles broad, and many others lefs. At the northern point of it, is one of thefe iflands, about two miles from the main land, which is a part of Mr. Hirzel's poffeffion. We came down to a few cottages on the fhore, which he has built, and where a floop lies always in readinefs to carry him over; into this we got,

leaving

leaving our horses in a barn by the cottage, and taking all our baggage with us in the vessel. In crossing the water, I was much delighted with the views; the hills in some places rise very boldly from the lake, which has a beautiful effect, as the whole country is covered with thick woods. The island is four miles long, and three broad, consisting of various land, but in general high and dry, and most of it a wood: Mr. Hirzel built a small house here, of four rooms on a floor, having two tolerable parlours, and the whole neatly furnished: in it we found a servant and his family, who has the management of a small farm: near it are barns, stables, and other offices; and four cottages, which he also built, and are inhabited by peasants; to each of whom he assigned a small farm, which he obliges them to cultivate very neatly. It is highly necessary that they should be good farmers; for the subsistence of themselves and cattle much depends on it, being at such a distance from any other habitation. Mr. Hirzel directs his own manager so, as to oblige him always to have good store of all products before hand. He has a cellar well filled, plenty of fish and game at command; and his farm yields him all common provisions, with good fowls: so that he is always sure of finding good eating and drinking: he has a large boat-house, under which his sloop can run; and several open boats. After dinner we took a walk about his farm, which seemed to be very well managed, and the crops good; at which I do not wonder; for the soil of the island is a fine black, dry, deep mold, peculiarly adapted, I should suppose, for all husbandry applications. As I had expressed a desire of sailing a little on the lake, for the pleasure of viewing the woods, Mr. Hirzel manned the sloop, in the morning of the 12th; and having laid in a stock of provisions and my bed, said, he would make a three days voyage for my entertainment; he steered south by the east shore, and returned by the west: we made many leagues, having a favourable wind, gaining very near the south end of the lake: nothing could be more agreeable; the water beautiful, and the surrounding country extremely various. We lived well; for his nets and hooks were excellently managed, and supplied us with many sorts of fine fish in great perfection, which we dressed and eat with an admirable stomach. We caught one carp that weighed sixteen pounds, and Mr. Hirzel told me that he has taken them of a larger size; but they are not so well tasted as those of about six or seven pounds. Here are

also

alfo pike, and tench, but not equal to what I have eat elfewhere; eels exceeding good; and a fifh about the fize of a trout, and of the fame fhape, but much fuperior flavour, which they call a *fnout*.—I muft confefs that this was one of the moft agreeable voyages I had ever made. We had about half a day in which the wind being brifk, the waves ran pretty high, and gave us the exercife of beating over them.

 The 15th, Mr. Hirzel dedicated to fhooting, for which fport we did not go off the ifland; he had a leafh of fpaniels there that found us plenty of game; thefe were pheafants and hares, with a few partridges; but none of them equal in tafte to the fame forts in England; we had a very good day's work to range about only a part of the ifland; and, having killed game enough for our ufe and amufement, returned home.

 Mr. Hirzel informed me that he had this ifland, which contains about eight thoufand acres of land, and a track contiguous to the cottages where we firft took water, of more than four thoufand more, by being the principal creditor of a man at Abo, who failed; they were valued at the price of the country, and rated to him for fomething more than three thoufand pounds; but he had them under five and twenty hundred, which is not four of our
           fhillings

shillings an acre for the fee simple, including all the fine woods on them. I expressed my astonishment at this; but he replied, that he had lost considerably by the purchase; having bought it for a country-seat for pleasure, that when he purchased it it did not yield a single shilling; and that the sums which he had hitherto laid out, did not much more than pay the interest of them. I answered, that still I should conceive the purchase might be made to answer extremely well, by improving the lands and converting them into farms: He said, no; he was very fearful that no money would arise, if it was all improved; for markets were at such an immense distance, that they could pay in nothing but products. But said he, I have hopes of making it answer another way. From the very southermost point of the lake, there is a considerable river which falls into the gulf of Finland; at the mouth of it there is a small trading town, which increases in shipping and commerce every day; upon that river there is a great forest, which belongs to a nobleman; and the merchants are employed at present in negotiating with him for liberty to cut what timber they please on his estate; if they succeed, they design to be at the expence of cutting a short canal to escape a fall, in order to carry down the timber to their

shipping;

shipping; if that is effected, there will be a navigation opened from this island into the gulf of Finland; and I shall possess a market at once for my timber, which will turn to greater account than any thing else that could be done; and after the timber is cleared, I can then apply it to husbandry-purposes, as the same market will carry my rents received in kind of tenants, or raised by myself to the same market as my timber. So that the moment the merchants succeed, my plan is to go and settle at Pitees, (the name of the town) that I may be on the spot, and I shall there, from superior advantages, be able to carry on a greater trade than at Waffay; besides the advantage of exporting the products of this estate. If I should ever be able to execute these plans, my purchase here will turn out the luckiest event of my life; and might soon enable me to buy larger tracks of land upon the lake; for most of the landlords live at Stockholm, and would know nothing of such a navigation being executed any more than of one in Iceland: for these tracks are all so desart, that very few of them yield any thing to their owners. But by my transferring my business to Pitees, I should be on the spot to make advantage of every event as it happened;

and

end it would be doubly advantageous to me, as I should be the exporter of my own products.

I asked him, if he did not apprehend the merchants would oppose any navigation but their own, as his timber would be brought to rival theirs? He replied, they could not; for the river is the boundary of the Russian and Swedish dominions, and is free by treaty; therefore the most that could be done would be the establishment of a small toll. That Pitees was part Swedish and part Russian, one part of the town being in Caulia, and the other in Nyland; which was found, in many circumstances of trade, to be a prodigious advantage, and was one reason of the town flourishing. I could not comprehend clearly how he made this out, for he did not explain himself. But it appeared evidently to me that he has a very fair chance of his purchase proving a fortune to him; and the plan he has laid for making the best of it, seems to be perfectly well considered.

It is astonishing to reflect on the vast importance of manufactures and commerce on the value of land: here are twelve thousand acres, most of them cover'd thickly with the finest timber bought for four shillings an acre the fee simple; the soil rich and fertile; materials for building of course, from the plenty of wood in the greatest profusion; a fine lake

lake well stored with quantities of fish, and the woods full of game: In a word, every article of provisions to be procured in the greatest plenty. But for want of manufactures and trade, the value is nothing—What would not such a track sell for in a well-peopled and industrious country; in England, Holland or France? This sufficiently shews the great consequence of population. I have heard it asked in England, when the decrease of our numbers has been the topic of discourse, of what consequence is the matter of population? It is plain, we have men enough for our armies and our navies; and our lands are cultivated; I have a thousand pounds a year, which does not fall to nine hundred, although our population it is said has suffered. And I must confess, that when I have heard such discourses, although I by no means approv'd their principle, yet did I not clearly see the consequences. This country supplies one with an answer at once. The rental of a private gentleman's estate depends on the sum total of the nation's population. If there are scarcely any inhabitants, as in these provinces of Sweden, the estate will sell for four shillings an acre timber and all; but if the country is full of inhabitants, like England, it will sell for twenty pounds, and the timber perhaps for two hundred more.

Between

Between such distant extremes there will certainly be many degrees, and some of them so near to each other, that it will be difficult to see their distinctions; but such are evidently in being, and must ever be found in proportion to the number of the people; if agriculture could alone find mouths enough to eat up and consume all the products she raises, then manufactures and commerce would not in this light be necessary; but it is every where known that a territory compleatly cultivated, will provide food &c. for a greater number of people than are employed in the cultivation: hence arises the deduction, that manufactures and commerce are but other names for full population, which can only be gained by their means.

From this island of my friend Mr. Hirzel, I was determined what route I should take to Petersburg: upon consideration, and after making many enquiries I resolved to go through the province of Savolax to the capital of it, the only town of any note in it, which is Nyslot; and thence to Wyburg in my way to the Russian capital. The 17th, in the morning I took my leave of Mr. Hirzel and his friend, and set off for Pexama, a little town at the distance of seventy miles; which is all through the forest: it took me two days; but I met

I met with no houses; therefore all my refreshment and rest was a meal taken on the grass, and a nap upon the same pillow. I have seen a Swedish map, which places seven villages in this road; but I had now sufficient reason to pronounce it erroneous: the country is all a rich soil, and covered in most places very thickly with fine timber: A country, which, would feed numerous inhabitants; and is all admirably watered; for I was more than once in sight of great lakes; but it is in the most desolate condition, and yields not any advantage to its possessors. From Pexama to Nyflot is between fifty and sixty miles; all the way on the banks of a very noble lake, which, from its narrowness and winding course, has exactly the appearance of a great river. The country is all forest; but I saw two or three villages; at one of which I took up my lodging: there were some small farms, which appeared to be tolerably cultivated; and I found that this lake, along which I had passed, was navigable quite to the gulph of Finland; and that the villages I saw were owing to this circumstance; for the timber of the forest was convey'd thither to advantage; and the cutting and preparing it found employment for the people.

Nyflet

Nyflot is a little neat town beautifully situated in a nook of land, that runs into the lake, with which it is chiefly furrounded. The church is a new building and handfome; the ftreets are fome of them well paved and tolerably built; and there was an appearance of wealth among the inhabitants, all of which I found was owing to the timber trade: for two or three miles round the town the country is well cultivated, and fhews plainly what the reft of it is capable of, did it poffefs the fame advantage of a market.

The 21ft in the morning I left Nyflot, and took the road to Wyburg, which is at the diftance of 60 miles: the firft day carried me into Caulia in the Ruffian territories, where I was forced to hire a frefh fervant to ferve me as an interpreter; but unfortunately I could only get a Ruffian, that underftood Swedifh, which language I began to fpeak a little: fo I hired him for the prefent ufe till I got to Petersburgh.

Upon entering the Ruffian territories, I was convinced, that the intelligence I had received at Waffay was true; that the Ruffians tempted the Swedes to fettle in their provinces, and at the fame time took all means of increafing the population of their dominions; for I not only faw and converfed with many Swedes,

Swedes, but the country was upon the whole well peopled with Ruffians, far fuperior to the Swedifh provinces in their beft diftricts that I have been in. All of it was cultivated, tho' not highly, and every thing carried the appearance of a thriving country, that had nothing to complain of. I arrived at Wyburg the 22d: it is a place of confiderable trade, which has increafed greatly of late years, by the encouragements it has received from the Ruffians. Vaft quantities of timber are exported from hence; fo that the harbour, which is a very good one, is feldom, while the fea is open, without many fhips in it. The provinces of Caulia and Kexholm furnifh this timber, and great quantities come from Savolax through a part of Sweden; this timber trade has increafed prodigioufly fince the Ruffians cut a fine canal to open a communication with the northern lakes, by which means trees are brought from the diftance of four hundred miles in rafts, and for a great part of the way five men are fufficient to bring down ten thoufand rafts.

The 23d I fet out for Peterfburg, which is two days journey, the diftance about fixty miles. The country, though fo near the capital of the Ruffian empire, is not all cultivated, which furprized me much; a great

Vol. III.   G   part

part of it confifts of forefts, and there are many marfhes; but ftill it is much fuperior to the Finland provinces of Sweden, better inhabited and better cultivated. But here it is time to take my leave of Sweden; however, I fhall add fome general obfervations I made on the people of that kingdom.

CHAPTER III.

General Reflections on the State of Sweden— Religion—Learning—The fine Arts—Manner of Life—Government—Agriculture— Manufactures—Commerce—Wealth—Population—Travelling.

THE common idea of the Swedes, which I have gathered from converfation and reading, has been that of their being good foldiers, active, brave, and hardy; but that few of them are ingenious, or have abilities to make a figure in other arts or walks in life. This has been owing to the actions that were performed by Charles XII. which were fuch proofs of their courage, that the reft of Europe too foon believed they were capable of being famous in war alone. I profefs myfelf clearly againft this idea, which I am confident is a very falfe one; they make

good

good foldiers it is true, but they are capable of making any thing elfe. I have attended with as much affiduity as I was able, and upon all the opportunities that I have had in my power, which have been many, I think they feem to have as good parts as any other nation in Europe, and much fuperior to fome. They are by no means dull of apprehenfion; are ready in their anfwers upon any fubject with which they are acquainted; have nothing of phlegm in their character: they are in general as chearful a nation as I know, not a noify buftling people that are one moment in grief and the next laughing : they have not fo much vivacity as the French, but I think they have, upon the whole, as much as the Englifh. They are in general a very patient and an induftrious people, and capable, with proper encouragement from the government, of making a great progrefs in the arts and fciences, and in manufactures and commerce; all which are very valuable qualities when they meet in a nation of fuch acknowledged bravery.

Refpecting religion, they are guided in a great meafure by plain good fenfe; though a free country, they are not peftered with noify fects ; neither are they at all violent in the conduct of the eftablifhed faith; and, altho'

a grea

a great part of the kingdom is very ignorant, yet I faw fewer figns of fuperftition than in any country I have been in, Holland and England alone excepted.

Among the better fort of people, and the higher ranks, there is a great deal of learning: a good education in Sweden fits a man to fhine in any country in Europe: in their fchools they learn Greek, Latin, French, Englifh, and German; fo that there are very few inftances of a young man's underftanding the dead languages, and not at the fame time being mafter of two or three very ufeful living ones, which is much more than can be faid of our youth in England.

They have feveral univerfities, which are provided with very able profeffors; in thefe feminaries, the favourite knowledge is natural hiftory and the mathematicks; and herein they fhew their good fenfe as much as any nation in Europe; for there are no other parts of knowledge that deferve fo much attention, the reft being for ornament alone; but thefe are ufeful in every branch of life. Many of their mathematicians are in general efteem, as they are very rarely without feveral whofe works are known to all Europe. In natural hiftory they are unrivalled; but they do not owe their fame in this branch

merely

merely to Linnæus, for before he was born, this ſtudy was the favourite one in their univerſities, and they have produced many men that gained them great reputation for their works, but they have ſince been eclipſed by Linnæus, and his numerous diſciples.

I have been in many mixed companies in Sweden, and I do not remember converſing with any gentleman that had not a conſiderable ſhare of knowledge, and plainly ſhewed on moſt topics that he had had the advantage of an excellent education.

They are moſt deficient in the polite arts; you look in vain for a painter, a poet, a ſtatuary, or a muſician. If the Abbeé du Bos's ſyſtem is a juſt one, this is the fault alone of their climate, but without attributing it to phyſical cauſes, we may find a reaſon in the moral ones. The fine arts never make a great progreſs in any country, till it becomes immenſely rich, and very luxurious: the arts are the children of luxury; without a great flow of expence running through every claſs of the people, we may pronounce that a nation is not rich enough for the fine arts to ſettle among them: the artiſts that excel muſt always be ſure of ſomething more than a competency, they muſt have affluence; they are generally men of warm imaginations, and lovers of pleasure. They must indulge their inclinations, and not be crampt in poverty, while they are attempting to produce works that shall be the admiration of succeeding ages. Hence all the famous ages in which the arts have risen to a great degree of eminence from many very famous men, being cotemporaries, have universally been the richest and most luxurious ages in the world: not that wealth is alone sufficient without luxury. The Dutch are very wealthy, but they are not a luxurious nation; artists would starve there in the midst of riches. Both luxury and wealth abound in the kingdoms of Asia, but then a despotism excessively severe, destroys every nobler effort of the mind.

The Swedes have no poets: some attempt that sort of composition, but it is always in Latin, and consequently of no merit: their painters never rise higher than very bad portrait ones: the same fashion obtaining in Sweden as in England, where till very lately we had nothing but portrait painters, because no others met with any encouragement. You hear very good music at Stockholm, but it is all by German musicians. This is not therefore a kingdom to which any person would resort to be entertained by the fine arts.

They

They have a theatre at Stockholm, on which, during a part of the year is represented French comedies, sometimes concerts, and oratorios, but the times of acting are very irregular; not meeting always with encouragement enough to keep it open even in the winter; so that it has been known to be shut up for two years together. Another thing which takes much from the gaiety of this capital, is, the court not being at all brilliant; which is owing in some measure to the smallness of the royal revenue, and to the present state of parties, which occasions many of the principal nobility to absent themselves.

The manners of all ranks of people in Sweden are very agreeable; the superior classes have an easy natural politeness, which prejudices you in their favour at first acquaintance. They have not a swift, or formal, nor pert or foppish, but a plain easy carriage and manner, which is the result of good sense and humanity. Their conversation is agreeable, and they pay great attention to foreigners, without troubling them with national customs and ceremonies. Duels are not common at Stockholm, yet the men have very just ideas of their honour; and as unwilling to put up with affronts as more tenacious and quarrelsome nations.

The principal expences into which they run, are thofe of the table, drefs, and equipage. People of large fortune keep prodigious tables, which are ferved with all the magnificence that is found in France and England, and the variety of their wines have no end. In drefs, alfo, they appear prodigal; and their equipages from their number are expenfive, but not executed in the fhewy tafte of Paris. However, thefe articles of luxury, in their greateft degree, are confined to a few families, whofe wealth is very confiderable; for in general the nobility are not rich: there are many private eftates in Germany that much exceed any in Sweden.

The way of dividing the refidence of winter and fummer, as practifed in England, takes place here only in part; many of the nobility and richeft of the gentry live entirely at Stockholm, fcarcely ever feeing their eftates; others live entirely in the country, never feeing the capital, at leaft but very feldom: fome, however, have houfes at Stockholm for the winter feafon, but live in fummer on their eftates, having very good houfes, which they ornament with gardens and plantations.

As to the prefent ftate of the government of Sweden, I could enter into a pretty long detail of fome changes and other circumftances

ces that have attended it lately, but as great part of my information is drawn from people that are deeply concerned, I do not chufe to fay much upon the fubject. But I fhall obferve that the government is a plain republick, the king being no more than the firft magiftrate with very little power, not fo much as a ftadtholder of Holland in feveral effential articles. There are convulfions in the adminiftration of affairs which threaten a total change; for here is an apparent contradiction, which is, a king and the people on one fide and the nobility on the other; moft of the important authority in the hands of the latter, who are in fact the legiflature of the kingdom; but difputes, parties and diffentions are grown to an amazing height, and bid fair for coming to open arms, at all events fome great revolution may be looked for; and the event may eafily be conjectured; while the people, united under a leader of the firft rank in the kingdom with fome prerogative, are on one hand, and the nobility on the other; a difpute in fuch a fituation cannot fail of being fatal to the latter. Indeed I never knew affairs in any country in a fituation that promifed fo fairly for bringing in an abfolute fway, in the fame manner as it was introduced in Denmark; many moderate men in Sweden

lament

lament the diffentions which do fo much mifchief to the kingdom, and affert that if they had a defigning prince on the throne it would be very eafy for him to feize as great a power as ever Charles XII enjoyed.

At the fame time that they are of this opinion, they make no fcruple to declare the change would be for the advantage of the kingdom, and that no government, regular in its operations, can be fo bad as the prefent irregular fcene of anarchy and faction. But herein they certainly carry their ideas to a very dangerous length notwithftanding many and great errors of government, and fome oppreffions among the peafants; yet I am clear, that the countrymen throughout the kingdom enjoy a great degree of liberty, and are left in quiet poffeffion of their property; their taxes are in fome inftances very unequal, they are kept at much diftance by the nobility, and have none of that licentioufnefs allowed them, which is fuch a difgrace to England: But, notwithftanding all thefe circumftances, I will venture to pronounce them beyond all comparifon, a happier people in every refpect than they would be, were their government abfolute. Let thofe who have travelled through France and Sweden, form an idea of the ftate of the peafants in both, and they will not

not for a moment hefitate at agreeing to this truth.

By lodging with the peafants in fo many journeys through the remote provinces of the kingdom, I had the opportunity of examining very minutely into their condition, and I remarked them in general to be a very contented happy people; there are few cottages in Sweden that have not lands annexed to them, by which means they raife many products which are of infinite ufe to them in keeping themfelves and families. England it will certainly be allowed, is as free a country as any man can wifh; and yet our labourers have very feldom more than a fmall fpot for a garden, which is too inconfiderable to be of much fervice to them; nor are the Englifh near fo well fatisfied with their lot as the Swedifh peafants; they are not fo tightly dreffed, their cottages are not near fo good, and their poverty in general, is much more apparent; all which I attribute to the circumftance of the Swedes having thofe fmall farms with herds of cattle on the wafte, which are of infinitely more value to them than all the amount of thofe taxes which they pay, and from which their brethren in England are not only exempted, but have alfo the advantage of rates publickly raifed for their affiftance;

ance; of which there is nothing of the kind in Sweden: I know not three peasants in that kingdom, that has not a farm of twenty or thirty acres of land at least, and several herd of cattle. Here indeed I should give an explanation, for if this was the case in England, we should have no such thing as a labourer to be hired; all would attend merely to their lands; but in Sweden there is no inconvenience in this, for the peasants who work regularly in the woods for hire have the same; but their wives and daughters manage their farms, so that the men are not taken from their usual labour three days out of forty. This is a most admirable custom for themselves, as well as the kingdom, and makes the population of a kingdom wherever it is practised, of far more account than at first it appears. It would be in vain to attempt introducing this custom into England, for the great degree of idleness in which the cottage-women live with us would be an unsurmountable obstacle.

Notwithstanding I have in different parts of my journal minuted the remarks I made on the present state of agriculture in the provinces I passed through; I must here repeat that the Swedes are universally good husband-men; I saw no lands laid out and cultivated

SWEDEN. 93

in such good order in any part of Germany, and the Danes are also far behind them; the peasants and farmers in Sweden who cultivate only for a subsistance, keep their lands in good order, and raise such crops, that their fields would be no disgrace to a midling cultivated part of England; while their farmers, as have good markets in view, would figure in the finest counties of this kingdom. Their crops of corn I observed were in general good and clean, that they keep large stocks of cattle, and provide plenty of food for them to subsist on in winter. If it is considered what a vast quantity of waste land is found throughout the kingdom, most of which almost any body that will take, may, under the payment of a very trifling rent; this good husbandry will appear the more extraordinary, as their having so much land in their power, it might be expected would make them slovens, yet the contrary is the case, for they take no more than they can manage well, and by that means I apprehend find their husbandry more profitable than it would otherwise be.

The reader may have remarked, that I have almost every where mentioned wheat being cultivated by them; this I think is a very extraordinary instance of docility and good
sense;

sense; a few years ago, that grain was cultivated only in a few of the southern provinces, and on soils picked with much care for it; but when the prohibition on the exportation from England put the Swedish government strongly on promoting the culture at home, the farmers throughout the kingdom readily came into the plan, and sowed so much every year, increasing the quantity regularly from that time to this, that at present it is spread all over the kingdom; such an instance, I dare to say, is not in any article of culture to be met with in England, and from this instance, it is very evident, that the common ideas of difficulties in the introduction of novelties, are many of them very false; for if any person had ventured to propose the culture of wheat in Sweden fifty years ago, at least, in many of the provinces where we now find it, he would have been thought mad; but none of these things can be well known, till a full and sufficient trial is made of them. The Swedes are now so well informed by experience in the culture of wheat, that some judicious and spirited laws would, I doubt not, enable them to raise quantities enough for a considerable exportation, so as to enable them to come in with the Poles for a share of a supply for the Dutch, and the

more

more southern nations of Europe: some bounties properly applied would effect this: not bounties as in England on the exportation, but to all those farmers who cultivated, given quantities of wheat in a certain round of years, on lands taken from the waste; for the great object is, the increasing the quantity of cultivated land, by improving the wild tracks, and at the same time applying them to raising a valuable sort of corn, that is sure to pay well for exportation. By making the grand object, the raising the corn instead of the exportation of it, the home consumption would always have the refusal at the market, which is not always the case in England. Laws should likewise be made to enable any peasant, farmer, or other, to take in as much of the waste which joins his farm, as he pleases, without paying any rent for twenty years, and afterwards only a moderate one for the life of the improver; this would be a wonderful encouragement to all the inhabitants of the country, and would certainly, in a few years bring great quantities of wheat to market; till the home consumption not taking the whole, a regular and profitable exportation, would of course be established. For bringing about such great works as these, nothing is wanted, but to bring affairs into

such

such a train, that private people, by pushing their own interests, must at the same time advance those of their country; for if ever there is a distinction made, nothing can arise from it but evil upon evil. Encouragement should also be given to the draining bogs and marshes, which in Sweden are universally the richest tracks to be met with, but this is a work beyond the power of most cultivators, without the assistance of the government; nothing would effect it but a premium of so much per acre, large enough to go far towards the whole expence, and if such premiums of whatever kind, amounted to a considerable expence, it should be raised by fresh taxes, or an increase of the old ones over the whole kingdom, for the benefit purchased would be of importance to the whole; and therefore the whole ought to contribute.

Nothing wants a wise regulation more than the woods in this kingdom; for the waste that is made in cutting them, both of timber and land, is extravagantly great. The attention which M. de Verspot has given to this article shews what should be done, and the manner also in which the undertaking should be prosecuted. No profitable woods ought to be destroyed, unless the land is converted immediately to husbandry uses. That nobleman's man's excellent method of thinning his woods is certainly the rational conduct, and ought to be inforced over the whole kingdom.

There is no country in which inland navigations would be attended with better confequences; for all their products are very bulky, and must have water-carriage, or they cannot be got to market. Many of the rivers of Sweden are navigable; but there are many tracks, covered with the finest woods, which yield scarcely any product, for want of water-carriage, at the same time that confiderable rivers run through them, which might at a very small expence be made navigable only by removing local obstructions, and not by a general deepening or widening.

Few countries are better supplied with harbours, many of which are extremely spacious and safe; and the number is so confiderable, that their trade will never stand still for want of them in any part of the kingdom.

Relative to the Swedish manufactures, I shall in general remark, that from what I viewed myself, and had intelligence of from others, they are not confiderable. Some of the nobility say, that they have carried their point, in making the Swedes cloath themselves

selves with cloth and linen of their own fabrick; but this is a very great exaggeration. The peasants are universally cloathed with a coarse woollen cloth that is made at home, and some other of the lower ranks of the people. There are also some gentlemen and nobles who, through patriotism, wear Swedish cloth that is pretty fine, but this is by no means general, and the cloth is much dearer than much finer sorts from England and France. These manufactories, which they have been able to erect, are not so considerable as this account may seem at first to indicate; for it should be remembered, that the peasants were always, nine parts in ten, cloathed in the same array as now, which is not with manufactory cloth, but with that which is spun, and wove in their own houses by their women; so that the new establishments are not very considerable; it is true, they increase, and, if good attention is given to encourage and protect them, they will in some years grow to be of very great consequence to Sweden, and not only entirely supply their own consumption with all except the fine French cloths, but also furnish coarse ones enough for exportation, in exchange for the finer sorts; and this will be pushing the advantage as far as ever they can

look

look for; but in the prefent ſtate of things they are far diſtant from this point, and, unleſs the animoſities which diſtract the government are ſo entirely laid aſide as to make all parties join in one work, and attend to that alone, viz. the good of the kingdom, there is no hope of their attaining to that deſirable ſtate.

They have ſome linen fabricks in which are wrought very good ſorts both of hemp and flax; but they are not near conſiderable enough to ſupply their home conſumption. Of glaſs and paper they import very little. Hard-ware is a conſiderable article among them, not in the ſtile of our Birmingham manufactures, but principally in the Foundery way: they caſt great numbers of cannon, which they export to all Europe; alſo bells in great number, and many other articles. Indeed, they are unrivalled in their iron and copper mines, which are far more conſiderable than thoſe of any other country in Europe; ſo that they apply copper to moſt of the purpoſes that we do lead in England, ſuch as coverings to their churches, publick buildings, and great private edifices, &c.

Commerce flouriſhes more in Sweden than it did ſome years ago: to what this is owing I could not diſcover, for their products are not greater in proportion to the increaſe of their shipping; and though several very judicious laws have been made for its encouragement, yet I should not have supposed the effect would have been answerable to what appears, unless other reasons had conspired at the same time. However, the fact is, that their shipping is much increased, their ships they build of a greater burthen, and they engage in more trading voyages than formerly. This is a point of very great importance; for, if they are able to export the principal part of their iron, timber, pitch, tar, hemp, and copper, in their own bottoms, it will add more than any thing else to the wealth of the kingdom, at the same time that their naval force will be increased greatly, which is the best and most useful force they can cherish. Increasing their shipping is improving and accelerating the markets for all their products, and cannot but increase them in a very high degree. The building and fitting out the ships is the most advantageous manufacture in the kingdom, and that which more than any other brings wealth into the country. The branches of commerce, which they have more particularly increased of late years, are the East-India trade, the trade to Portugal, Spain, and the Mediterranean; that of England, Holland, and France, is not improved. Some persons are in doubt about

the

the German branch of their commerce, but I believe that is rather greater than it was.

The general effects, which flow from an improving agriculture and increaſing manufactures and commerce, are a greater degree of national wealth, more of the precious metals, and an increaſing population. From the beſt intelligence I could get, the kingdom I believe is more wealthy than it was twenty years ago. It contains more money, and is upon the increaſe in that article; but as to population it has made no progreſs, and many perſons affirm that there is a decline in it. How far this is conſiſtent with the improvement in the other particulars I ſhall not determine; but I may remark, that in general thoſe circumſtances are attended by an increaſing people. What cauſes ſhould have wrought contrary effects in Sweden I am not able to aſcertain; but, as the people are often numbered, (though not accurately, nor all the claſſes) the fact is pretty well confirmed. It ſhould make one doubt the extent of thoſe improvements; for I muſt own I have little idea of agriculture, manufactures, and commerce improving, without population increaſing exactly in the ſame proportion; for an increaſing people can only be owing to the inhabitants finding an eaſe in maintaining themſelves, and their families no burthen,

burthen, which is effected by a great plenty of employment; and improving agriculture, manufactures, and commerce, is increasing employment, and consequently the people.

Travelling in Sweden, unless upon the system which I followed, is a very uneasy affair, the moment you get out of the few great roads there are, which do not lead through a fifth of the kingdom; but in these, if you have your own carriage, the post-horses, boys, and accommodations, have nothing objectible in them, and you are sure of meeting with great civility in all the inns, and from every person with whom you have the least connection on the road. But, when you leave these great roads, then the stage in distance from inn to inn is very great, and the accommodation, though with much civility, very indifferent. If your bed is carried with you, and you can ride the whole journey, every peasant's house is open to you with the utmost hospitality; and they will for very trifling rewards do whatever is in their power to serve you. Without precautions, the diet will be very indifferent; but they will get you fish, wild fowl, and venison, excellent of the kind, with which you may load a horse from place to place while it keeps. And this will remedy every inconvenience. Wine is easily carried.

Travels through Ruffia.

CHAP. IV.

Description of Peterſburg—General Accounts of the Empire of Ruſſia—The Empreſs—Government—Manufactures—Trade—Army—Navy—Preſent State.

I Arrived at Peterſburg the evening of the 24th. and, as I deſigned making ſome ſtay in the city, determined to hire private lodgings; for I had been informed that the publick inns were not only very extravagant, but alſo very bad, which indeed is the caſe in all capitals, for, where the people of quality do not go, (having houſes of their own) one is always ſure of meeting with very indifferent treatment. I hired a firſt floor, conſiſting, after the Ruſſian faſhion, of two dining-rooms, a drawing-room, dreſſing-room, and bed-chamber, beſides ſervants' apartments, for three guineas a week; ſuch a ſuit of rooms as at London it would be very difficult to have at twelve. Peterſburg is built on ſeveral iſlands, which were once nothing more than marſhy ſpots of mud over-run with reeds: but the immortal Peter, whoſe undertakings in every thing carried a magnificence of idea in them that can never be ſufficiently admired, converted a miſerable bog into a fine city.

And

And here I cannot avoid anfwering the reflections of feveral writers againft that immortal monarch, for facrificing more than half a million of men in founding this city. The Czar's object was to become an European Power, which without a port on the Baltick he might as well have pretended to be an American one. His vaft dominions, though contiguous to Poland, and themfelves a part of Europe, were at fuch a diftance from the European theatre, and in fo barbarous a ftate, that nothing but opening himfelf a way to the Baltick could poffibly bring his grand plan to bear. By founding this city, and making it the capital of his empire, and a fea-port fit to receive the naval force he deftined to act on that fea, he anfwered all his purpofes at one ftroke; and confequently could fcarcely pay too dearly for the propofed advantage. As to the lofs of fuch numbers of lives, the fault certainly was not fo much owing to the fteadinefs of the Czar's adhering to his plan, as to not taking proper care of the men while they were at the work, fince every one muft be very fenfible that works, to the full as great as any he executed, could now be performed in England under fimilar circumftances, comparatively fpeaking, without the lofs of a man. But the confequences, which

we

we all know have flowed from the founding this city, have been of such infinite importance to the Russian empire, that no expence that could ever have been incurred would have been too great for gaining such signal benefits. Petersburg is the soul of commerce in all these Northern parts; it is the foundation on which all the Russian naval force has been erected; and the port, on which most depends their nursery of sailors. At the same time that these capital circumstances attend it, it must be acknowledged that it is very deficient as a receptacle of the men of war of a great empire; for the depth of water, the freshness of it, the docks, yards, every thing at Petersburg, are against the use of it for that purpose. The yards are at Petersburg, but the depth of water is so inconsiderable that nothing can be put aboard the first-rate men of war before they are conveyed to Cronslot, which is not easily done neither. Once this work was effected by means of most expensive machines, but now they come without that difficulty by means of the new canal, which is not however so complete but that infinite attention is necessary for conducting them. It is not only men of war, however, that are built in these yards: galleys * are much

* Count Algarotti, mentioning the naval power of the Russians,

much in use for the Baltick; but, as this empire has experienced of late great changes, in the Russians, observes, "Galleys are here the proper things. Be there never so little water, there is always enough for them. They glide between the little islands and the rocks; they can land any where. The Czar was sensible of it at last, and sent for galley-builders from Venice. I met with one of them greatly advanced in years, and was not a little surprised to hear terminations in *as* in sixty degrees of latitude. The galleys that one sees here are of different sizes; there are small ones, which carry about one hundred and thirty men, and others much larger. They are all armed with two pieces of cannon on the prow, and furnished with chace-guns and swivels on the sides. The Czar gave to each of them the name of a Russian fish. Now they are numbered as the legions were; there are upwards of one hundred and thirty of them, and they are to be much more numerous. By this means an army of thirty thousand men is transported with great ease. Rowing is to the Russian soldiers what the exercise of swimming was to the Romans. Every foot-soldier learns to handle the oar at the same time as the musket, by which means, without maritime commerce, and without embargoes, the Russians have always crews ready for their galleys. They cast anchor every night, and land where it is least expected. When disembarked, they draw them up upon the land, range them in a circle with their prows and artillery pointed outward, and thus they have in a trice a fortified camp. They leave five or six battalions to guard it, and with the rest of their troops over-run the country, and lay it under contribution. The expedition ended, they re-embark, and begin again in another quarter. Sometimes they transport their vessels from one water to another over a slip of land, as was practised by the antients on several occasions, and particularly the syftem of politicks, the ufe of galleys vary. In a war on the coaft of the Baltick they are increafed in number; but, when a peace comes, they are neglected, and not kept up indeed in the manner they ought to be. During the late war, they might have annoyed the Pruffian dominions infinitely more than they did; but the great army was the only thing attended to.

Peterfburg is amazingly increafed in fize within thefe forty years: At the death of Peter the Great, it did not contain eighty thoufand

cularly after the example of Mahomet II. at the fiege of Conftantinople.

" The Swedes can teftify whether thefe Ruffian galleys are formidable. They have feen them ravage their rich mines of Norkopping, the whole coafts of Gothland and Sudermania, and fhew themfelves even before Stockholm."——He alfo adds another circumftance, which is worthy of note, concerning the timber ufed for fhipbuilding here.———" Of what wood do you think the fhips are built at Peterfburg ? It is a fpecies of oak which is at leaft two fummers upon the road before it arrives. It comes ready cut by the carpenter from the kingdom of Cafan. It goes a little way up the Wolga, then the Tuertza, paffes through a canal into the fea, from thence into the Mefta, and by means of the Volcova falls into a canal which conveys it into the lake Ladoga, from thence it defcends at laft by the Neva to Peterfburg. I faw in this port a floop built at Cafan, from whence it came by the rivers I have juft mentioned, which join the Cafpian fea to the Baltick, and are a quite different thing from the famous canal of Languedock."

thoufand inhabitants, and now the Ruffians affert that there are five hundred thoufand, but this is an exaggeration. It covers a very great extent of land and water; the ftreets are fome of them very broad, long, and with canals in the middle of them; and others are planted in the Dutch fafhion, which I before obferved is a wretched plan; the houfes are immenfely large: the palaces of the nobility, I think exceed in fize thofe of any city I have feen; and that of the Emprefs is an amazing ftructure; but let me remark that they are rather great than beautiful: the fize is all that ftrikes you: and thefe prodigious piles are ftuck fo thick with ornaments, that there is hardly any fuch thing as judging of their proportions: the Italian architecture is mixed with the Dutch, and the whole forms very inelegant buildings, in which true tafte is totally facrificed to a profufion of ornament. But if the eye does not fcrutinize into the feparate parts of the buildings, but takes only the ftreets at large, the city may be fairly pronounced a very fine one.

The Czar himfelf fpared no pains in rendering it as ftrong as poffible; for being at the very extremity of his dominions, clofe to his enemies the Swedes, and open to the attacks which were poffible to arife from his European connections,

connections, he made a point of having it impregnable; but herein he certainly failed. There are many forts and whole shores converted into platforms, and lined from end to end with great guns. These works begin at Cronflot, which is made very strong, and they last to the city. There is a citadel regularly built, and capable not only of protecting the city on one side, but also itself of standing a siege. Yet there are many seamen who assert that a fleet of ships well manned and conducted, and provided with a proper number of fireships, and bomb-ketches, would without any great difficulty lay all Peterburg in ashes. I must own myself of a very different opinion, for here is always a very confiderable fleet of men of war, from 60 to 100 guns, with numerous sailors, that could man them on a very short notice; these ships properly disposed by way of batteries, would render such an attempt impracticable, even if the fortifications are granted to be deficient, which is more than will be allowed by many officers well skilled in this part of their art.

Among the publick buildings, there are many extremely worthy the attention of a traveller, particularly the dock yards and naval magazines, the arsenal, foundery, admiralty, &c. without infifting on the imperial palace, the

the cathedral, or many churches. In the docks they have a great number of carpenters continually at work, among whom are many Englifh, difcharged by the government on the conclufion of the peace in 1763, they meet with great encouragement here, and are much better employed than if in the fervice of France or Spain. They build here all forts of veffels, from fhips of one hundred and twenty guns, (and fome much larger have been known) down to boats, and the number always on the ftocks at a time is confiderable. After the death of Peter the Great the marine was neglected, infomuch, that the Emprefs's naval ftrength was not computed to be a fifth part of what that great monarch poffeffed, and this was owing to a want of trade, which can alone make feamen; unlefs when in the hands of fuch a man as Peter, who created every thing: But the prefent Emprefs, who has thrown the fpirit of that great monarch into all the departments of the ftate, has revived it wonderfully, fo that at prefent the Ruffians have a formidable navy, and in a few years will have a yet more confiderable one.

There is fcarcely any thing at Peterfburg more deferving notice than the foundery: The iron is brought from Kexholm by water, and

and the number of cannon and mortars that are cast here is very great; also cannon balls, shells, and all sorts of military implements in which iron is used; which are made here at as small an expence as in Sweden, or any other part of the world. The arsenal is always well stored with them; and there are vast quantities made on a private account for exportation, forming a very confiderable branch of commerce.

The trade of Petersburg is much more confiderable than that of any other town in the Russian empire; and would figure on comparison with many very great marts in other parts of Europe, but unfortunately that vast commerce is nine-tenths of it carried on in foreign bottoms. The Dutch alone load annually here with timber, iron, and all sorts of naval stores a great many ships, and the English many more.

The commodities these nations carry from Petersburg are tar, bees wax, pitch, hemp, flax, leather, skins, furs, pot-ashes, timber, plank, iron, yarn, linen, lintseed &c. and these in such quantities that the very ballance of trade between Great-Britain and Russia has been reckoned at four hundred thousand pounds a year against the former; the amount of the total commerce may therefore be easily conceived. The royal navy of England

land is almost totally supplied with hemp from Petersburg, great quantities of iron, and other naval stores, and all the shipping in England likewise; and this importation has increased very much since the Swedes laid a prohibition on our manufactures, so that the importation from that country was reduced to the few articles which necessity obliged us to have from thence; and all the rest very politically transferred to Russia.

The great amount of the commerce between us and this empire has been the occasion of very many political dissertations and treatises proving the necessity of encouraging the production of all the commodities we import from Russia, in our colonies; and I think our politicians have not in any instance had better grounds for their opinions, or supported their propositions with more unanswerable arguments. A trading nation should never regret parting with its money when she thereby adds to her industry; but in this case we pay three or four hundred thousand pounds a year to Russia for those commodities which our own colonies would produce; and the difference is that now we pay in cash, but to our colonies we should pay in manufactures: consequently, for want of this measure being effected, we lose the employment

ployment of so many of our poor as could earn the whole amount of that sum; and we also lose the general profit resulting to the nation at large by their earning such a sum of money; for any increase of our national income raised by an increase of industry, is beneficial to us in a much greater degree than the mere amount of it. To illustrate this, let us consider the advantage to Russia of our paying her a ballance of three or four hundered thousand pounds. That ballance is paid to a certain number of merchants and dealers at Petersburg and other ports; they pay it to a set of landlords, miners, husbandmen, and manufacturers. These again pay it to all the manufacturers, tradesmen, &c. with whom they deal; and these to a fresh set. Now every art, trade, business, and profession in the whole empire come in for an additional income from this sum circulating through the mass of industry; and every one of them are essentially the richer. If this circulation could be traced, it would probably be found, that three hundred thousand pounds a year gained in the precious metal, were equal in general improvement to the value of nine or twelve hundred thousand pounds a year. Because no one can be supposed to have an increase of income in Russia, any more than any where elſe, without increaſing his expences proportionably; that is, he buys more food, more cloth, more ſhoes, employs more builders, and, in a word, more artiſts of all ſorts. None of which can increaſe without reciprocal benefits flowing back again; and the government from the whole circulation in every ſtep it takes ſeizes a part by means of taxes. This is but a ſlight ſketch of the effects of an increaſing wealth; to explain it fully would take a much greater compaſs.

The greateſt trade at Petersburg is carried on by the Engliſh; next in rank come the Dutch; as to the French, they deal here as little as poſſible; for the two crowns are very far from being on a good footing, the French and the Swedes being in cloſe alliance, they therefore trade to Sweden for all thoſe commodities which England gets from Ruſſia, ſome few excepted, which are not to be had at that market. Notwithſtanding this, they conſume large quantities of French commodities in Ruſſia, but theſe come to them principally through the hands of the Dutch.

The building this capital has had a very great effect in improving large tracks of land in the ſurrounding provinces: The corn and other proviſions which are brought hither,

ther, and the variety of merchandize that is exported from hence, employ fome of the moft confiderable inland navigations in the world. The Neva, the great lakes of Lagoda and Onega; the Tuerka, the Mefta, the Volcova and the Wolga, all thefe rivers, with many others, tho' fome of them are at a great diftance, keep open a communication between Petersburg and thofe noble tracks of country upon the Cafpian and Euxine feas: but it may be fuppofed that the greateft advantages are made by the people who have not fuch a diftance to go; fo that the products of all the neighbouring provinces are infinitely greater that thofe of others more diftant.

I have heard fome Ruffians affirm, that all this feeming increafe of culture, of manufactures, and of commerce, is imaginary, that it is all owing to the fovereign's fixing the feat of government here, which has not raifed a new population, but drawn an old one from other provinces. Mofcow was once the metropolis, and the feat of government, &c. and Novogorod the great ftaple of trade, but Petersburg now is both; and has half depopulated thofe cities, as well as Archangel, which was once a place of very great trade. In anfwer to this I allow, that part of the affertion is true; that much of the population of this city, and its neighbourhood, is owing to a defertion of other places; but at the fame time I muft infift, that a new population muft have been created by means of this city, becaufe a new induftry has fprung up, new trades opened, new manufactures eftablifhed, and innumerable artifts employed, which were not in being before; and many of which could not have been in being had not this city been founded. There is no doubt, but the Ruffian commodities found, in fmall quantities, their way into Europe before Peter the Great's time; but every one muft be fenfible of the comparative fmallnefs of the quantity when they had not an European port, and when all their products, in order to get to the Baltick, were forced to fubmit to a long land carriage through an enemy's country, and fubject to whatever duties that enemy chofe to lay on them. The prefent method of carrying on their trade, manufactures and products has I think every advantage over the former; and if this is allowed, it follows of courfe, that population is proportionably increafed, and wealth moft certainly; both which have a direct effect in raifing the value of land for a great diftance around the capital.

But the building of the city was a work of
the

the Great Peter's, which is giving it all the illuſtration that is neceſſary; for if ever mortal was endowed with the true art of governing, with that kind of univerſal genius equally great in practice and ſpeculation, it was him. All his ideas, all his plans had ſomething ſo great and comprehenſive in them; ſuch a power of foreſeeing future events, and ſuch abilities in providing for them, that he never once failed in theory, tho' in practice obſtacles ſometimes aroſe which were beyond his power to counteract. The founding of Peterſburg is one capital inſtance; for ever ſince he made it the ſeat of his marine, and the principal trading town of his dominions, it has been of more real ſervice to the empire than any other meaſure he could poſſibly have adopted. What an extent of political imagination is diſplayed in his inland navigations! They have a greatneſs unrivalled in any other part of the world. But the moſt capital project of the Czar's was that wherein he planned a navigation to the Mediterranean.—Next to Petersburg the favourite of his empire was Azoph, the reaſon of which was his deſign of eſtabliſhing a trade from thence thro' the Thracian Boſphorus to the Archipelago. This would not only have given him greater mercantile advantages than Petersburg,

but

but would have endangered the very being of the Turkish empire; by letting a naval power of the Ruffians into the very heart of Conftantinople; and that Peter defigned fomething more than commerce, we may eafily gather from his forming docks, yards, and naval magazines, at Azoph; and actually had fhips of feventy guns upon the ftocks, which fufficiently fhewed that he intended a naval war upon the Euxine fea againft the Turks.

The Ruffian empire, though of fuch an amazing extent, is very well known to be badly peopled. The beft writers inform us, that it contains feventeen millions of inhabitants, and one million in the conquered provinces; but from the beft accounts I could get at Petersburg, I believe the number at prefent to be more confiderable. Almoft from the moment that the prefent emprefs began to reign, fhe has increafed the number of her fubjects by many ways, principally by a general and very active encouragement of all arts, of agriculture, mining, manufactures and commerce, and this with fuch effect, that all of them are more flourifhing at this time by many degrees than they were twenty years ago. And another means which fhe has taken to increafe her people has been inviting foreigners;

this

this she has done in a still greater degree than any of her predecessors; almost from her acceffion to the empire she has brought continual bodies of Germans, Poles, and Greeks from Turkey, to settle in her dominions, and these not few in numbers; from the coasts of Germany ship loads, but from Poland and Turkey whole towns, villages and districts have left their habitations and settled in Russia; nor has it been only at certain times, but regular emigration in consequence of her continued encouragement.

This encouragement which the Empress has constantly granted consists in several very important articles. All the expences of the journey, or voyage from their native country, are borne by her; she feeds and supports them by the way. Upon their arrival at the territory appointed them to cultivate (which has always been part of the crown lands) every family has a cottage erected at her expence, to which they contribute labour; they then are furnished with implements necessary for cultivation, and one year's provisions for the whole family. A further advantage is an exemption from all taxes during five years. All which is a system of such admirable policy, and carried into execution with such unusual spirit, even while the finances of the empire have been

been much diftreffed by expenfive wars, that I know not an inftance in hiftory fuperior to it. There can be no doubt but the advantages muft be immenfe, not only in population, but alfo revenue; for thefe fettlers, though they have an affignment of lands for ever, yet it is, after a certain number of years, under payment of an annual quit-rent, fufficient to produce a confiderable revenue. The continued diforders in Poland, and the oppreffions in Turkey, have caufed many thoufands of families annually to leave their country, and make ufe of this bounty of the emprefs. By this time the increafe of people muft be very great; fome perfons, whofe information I believe is very good, affured me, that the number of fouls thus gained, fince the acceffion of the prefent Czarina, is not lefs than fix hundred thoufand; I muft own the number appears almoft incredible. We may, without fuppofing the total fo very great, eafily fee from hence that fhe muft have raifed the revenue of the crown lands very much, and put them in a way of being yet more improved; for certainly peopling them was the firft rational ftep that could be taken, and one which never could deceive her. I made enquiries concerning the fituation of the emigrants, and whether all the promifes that

had

had been made to them had been executed, and I was aſſured that they were moſt punctually; but that in very many caſes much more was done for them than promiſed, and every effort taken to make them perfectly ſatisfied with their choice; a proof of which is the increaſed numbers that have been coming from the beginning: the accounts ſent back by the firſt ſettlers, being ſuch as induced others to take the ſame meaſures, and this effect has been regular ever ſince, ſo that the number of new comers is at preſent greater than ever, and promiſes to be ſo conſiderable, that in a few years, if the troubles in Poland continue, the increaſe of people here will be immenſe, and with them certainly that of the power, and wealth of the empire. Nor has any event of her reign diſcovered a greater underſtanding than this regular favour ſhewn to population.

The revenues of the Ruſſian empire are very great, conſidering the value of money; which in theſe ſort of diſquiſitions ought ever to be conſidered, though it rarely is ſo. The Empreſs is in many articles the ſole merchant in her dominions. The whole trade by land to China is on her account: this is not indeed conſiderable, for a carravan rarely goes now. Rhubarb, pot-aſhes, and ſpices, are branches in which ſhe, and no body elſe, trades.

trades. Salt is an article that brings her in an immense revenue. Very large quantities of the best hemp of the Ukrain are bought and sold on her account; much iron, the same; and even beer and brandy are her's. Besides these articles, she has customs, tolls, and a poll-tax of three shillings and six-pence a head. The crown-lands, which are prodigiously extensive, bring in a considerable revenue.

The following general account was shewn me at Petersburg of the Empress's revenue, reckoned in English money. It is handed about there, and thought to be not very far from the truth in any article.

Poll-tax	1,750,000
Crown-lands	672,000
Salt	542,000
Hemp and iron	370,000
China trade Rhubarb and Spices	48,000
Pot-ashes	60,000
Customs	179,000
Baths and licensed houses	68,000
Other duties &c. comprehending all other taxes	400,000
Total	£ 4,089,000

But the value of such a revenue will not appear

appear clearly to any reader, that does not confider the great difference of the value of money in this country, and others that are full of commerce and wealth; upon the nearest computation I can make, thefe four millions are about as good as ten in England. And if we fuppofe them ten, we fhall then fee the great importance of liberty, trade and manufactures in raifing a publick revenue; for eighteen or nineteen millions of people in Ruffia, yield no greater revenue than a third of that number yield in England. Wealth therefore depends no further on population than the induftry of that population extends. It is a flourifhing agriculture, improving manufactures, and an extenfive commerce which yield a great publick revenue. Introducing induftry among all claffes of people that were not induftrious before, is therefore as effential an increafe of inhabitants as bringing in foreign emigrants: both thefe means have been employed by the prefent fovereign of Ruffia, for the aggregate of the induftry of this empire is vaftly more confiderable than when fhe came to the throne.

She has iffued out feveral edicts for the encouragement of agriculture; and herein fhe has proceeded with her ufual politicks; for fhe rightly confidered that the way to make this
moft

most useful of all the arts to flourish is to set its professors at ease; she has accordingly given a much greater degree of liberty to the peasants than ever they enjoyed before; for they were greater slaves than even in Poland; but now every nobleman (called yet Boyards in Russia) whose estate consists of a given number of families, is obliged to enfranchise one family every year, and they are directed by the Empress to select for this purpose the most industrious family they have: the peasant has a farm assigned him, and the Empress makes him a present of some implement of the greatest use; but he is by the same edict to pay after three years a rent to the nobleman that is very considerable; the design of which is to convince the nobility of the advantage of letting their estates to the peasants to be paid a rent in money: and I was informed that many of them had made a great progress in it, partly from conviction of its expediency, and partly from paying their court to the sovereign.

Besides this measure, there are great encouragements given both in freedom, and in exemption from taxes and services, to all those who improve waste lands, by bringing them into culture. Such a system is highly necessary in an empire that contains more land than Europe, but not more inhabitants than Germany;

Germany; and where immenſe tracks of as fine ſoil as any in the world are utterly waſte. If the life of the preſent Empreſs is a long one, great things will be done in this walk of improvement, and many very extenſive territories cultivated which have hitherto laid waſte. The foreigners which ſhe has ſettled, and continues to ſettle, and the encouragement which huſbandry meets with, will have a great effect in giving a new countenance to the agriculture of many provinces.

 I made enquiries concerning the preſent ſtate of Ruſſian manufactures, and was informed that they have never been able to make them any thing conſiderable: They have at Peterſburg ſome very large founderies, where all ſorts of ammunition and military ſtores are made; and they make ſome very good cloth of hemp, but the quantity of this laſt is not conſiderable. There are many other fabricks, but not of conſequence, nor any ways proportioned to the number of the people. They have many woollen manufactories, but they do not cloath even their own army. England has the greateſt ſhare in the commerce of ſupplying them; the import at Peterſburg of coarſe and fine woollen cloths is very conſiderable: what we do not ſend them, they have from the Dutch; but the French
ſend

send none. Nor is there hardly a manufactory in England that does not send great quantities of its fabricks hither; and notwithstanding so great an exportation, yet the importation of hemp, iron, &c. is so great, that a large ballance is paid (as I before mentioned) to Russia. There are several instances of much encouragement being given to the national manufactures, but the effect has not been great, and I must own myself of opinion that it never will be great, for the Russian do not seem to take to any sort but those in which they are from their infancy conversant. They make excellent carpenters, ship-builders, smiths, and founders, but they will never make a figure as weavers.

It also deserves enquiry, whether it would be highly political to make any great efforts in complicated manufactures which require very many hands, while there is so immense a territory to cultivate, and not of barren mountains like Sweden, but of great extended plains of as rich land, as the best parts of England, or even Holland: consequently with such materials to work upon, it is much to be questioned if a given number of hands would not in raising hemp and flax, or making potashes, bring in a greater sum of money to the country, than if they were employed in manufactures.

nufactures. It appears to me very clearly that they would. From the defcriptions which I have had of feveral immenfe provinces of this empire, I have no doubt but a thoufand pounds and ten people would, employed in attending cattle, yield a greater return in hides and tallow alone; than from any manufactures they could be employed in; for there are meadows (not bogs or marfhes) covered with fine grafs of an hundred fquare miles in a place, with no other inhabitants than what are wild, and very few of them. In a country where there is fuch plenty of excellent land, and through which run fo many navigable rivers that would convey all its products to a ready market; and notwithftanding thefe advantages, there are large waftes ftill on the very banks of thofe rivers—under fuch circumftances I apprehend, that no attention to manufactures can yield a profit equal to a proper cultivation: the wealth arifing from it would be far greater, the publick revenue would be much more improved, and population increafed in a much greater proportion. If I was fufficiently verfed in the theory of ftocking ground with inftruments of tillage, and with cattle, &c. I fhould be able to make this appear by minute calculations; but I do not

not apprehend that there is any reafon in general to doubt it.

While this is the cafe, whoever fills the throne of Ruffia will moft advance the interefts of that empire by promoting, by every poffible means the cultivation of fo immenfe a territory; if there happens a fuccffieon for a long period of time of fuch fovereigns as at prefent fill that throne; this vaft empire will be raifed by thefe means to a pitch of grandeur, much exceeding what it at prefent poffeffes: and from the conduct which has been hitherto purfued by the prefent Emprefs, there is great reafon to think that fhe is fenfible of the importance of directing her views principally to this end; they have hitherto been attended with fuch fuccefs, as to be a very ftrong proof that the plan upon which fhe has proceeded, is a juft one; a different one might have been followed more in favour of manufactures, by planting the foreign emigrants thickly in the near neighbourhood of thofe places only which have fabricks in them; with a view to the employment of many of them in thefe manufactures.

Relative to the commerce of Ruffia, it fhould be remembered previoufly to any enquiry into its prefent ftate, that this immenfe empire is by no means fituated advantageoufly

for

for trade. The only ports that it poſſeſſes, from which any trade of conſequence can be carried on, are in the Baltick, a ſea that is frozen almoſt half the year; and, at the ſame time, it is at the extremity of the empire; ſo that the commodities, which are exported through this ſea, are obliged to be brought ſome thouſands of miles before they are put on board the ſhips. This is ſuch a diſadvantage, that it much affects the commerce of the empire, and is of a nature that will not admit of any remedy. This circumſtance conſidered, the commerce of Ruſſia is very conſiderable, as to the export of its products and commodities, but the ſhipping of the empire is very trifling compared with that to which ſhe gives employment. All the trade which the Engliſh carry on with Ruſſia is in their own bottoms; it is the ſame with the Dutch, and almoſt all other European nations; ſo that the Ruſſian flag is ſcarcely known in the world, although Ruſſian commodities are met with in ſo many places.

To remedy this evil by a general extenſion of commerce, and by procuring a navigation on a more favourable ſea, the Czar Peter the Great formed the noble plan of raiſing a naval power on the Black ſea, and eſtabliſhing a commerce on it, with a communication thro' the sea of Constantinople with the Mediterranean; one of the greatest designs which could have entered the head of any sovereign of Russia, and which would give a very considerable share of the commerce of the world to that empire. It should be remembered, that the richest products which Russia exports are those of the most southernly provinces, particularly the Ukraine; which is universally allowed to be one of the finest countries in the world; the rivers which flow through this territory all take their course to the Black sea; so that it is only by an artificial navigation, and a long land carriage that they are brought to Petersburg. It is well known that they could be delivered at Constantinople for a much less price than at Petersburg; which, with the increase of trade resulting from a navigation open all the year, and immediately into the center of Europe, would give the empire at one stroke, ten times the commerce. it can ever possess otherwise; and would, at the same time, give the Czarina such an advantage over the Turks, as to endanger the very existence of Constantinople, and with it that of their empire. And if the plan upon which that great monarch conducted his wars against the Turks be considered, it will appear that he never lost sight of this great object. Azoph

was

was the town which he acquired at a very great expence of men and money: he fortified it at a yet greater expence, and built a fleet of ſtout ſhips for that navigation, with docks, yards, and magazines of all ſorts; but the unfortunate campaign of the Pruth put an end to his hopes, and gave back that conqueſt to the Turks. Had he been ſucceſsful, he deſigned the conqueſt of the Crimea, which would at once have given him poſſeſſion of a noble province, and the command of the Euxine. The ſame idea was ſteadily purſued in the war of 1735, which ended with the ceſſion of Azoph to the Ruſſians, a fortreſs of all others the moſt important for the proſecution of this deſign.

A very little reflection will give us an idea of ſome of the conſequences which would, in all probability, attend the execution of this plan. Without ſuppoſing an entire conqueſt of Moldavia, Bulgaria, and Walachia, with the Tartar diſtricts to the North of the ſea, as ſome writers have done, let us only ſtate the navigation from the Euxine to the Mediterranean being made free to both nations, and Azoph and the Crimea in the hands of the Ruſſians. They would then have a free navigation from all parts of their empire, by

means

means of the Tanais and the Donetz, down to Azoph; that port would then be the grand magazine of all the commodities of their empire, where their ships would load for diftributing them through all the fouthern countries of Europe, and on the coaft of Africa, at the fame time that Petersburg fent them to all the Northern ones. But this trade would give them a new export, which would prove perhaps of more confequence than all the others put together; that of corn: the fineft territories of Europe for husbandry are faid to be the tracks on the North of the Black fea, including their province of the Ukraine; at prefent thefe countries have no vent for fuch a product, and therefore raife no more than for their own confumption; but, in cafe of fuch a Ruffian navigation as I am now fpeaking of, this teritorry would lie much better for fupplying the beft corn markets in Europe, than thofe which at prefent fupply them. Barbary and Sicily it is true yield an uncertain fupply; but it is well known that Holland fupplies moft of the demands of Portugal, Spain and Italy, when embargoes are laid in England; and the Dutch bring the corn they thus trade in from Dantzick; let the reader therefore compare the navigation from Azoph, to all the coafts of the Mediterranean, with that from

from Dantzick, round three fourths of Europe. It is very evident, that the Ruffians would at once command the entire fupply of all thofe countries; not only with fo important an article as that of corn, but would, for the fame reafon, gain the exclufive trade of naval ftores to them likewife; iron, hemp, canvafs, timber, &c.

Relative to ftrength in war, the fuccefs of fuch a plan would only be too great; for one can hardly fuppofe the Turks would fubmit to a Ruffian navigation through the heart of Conftantinople, without they were firft reduced to the laft extremity; and in fuch a ftate of weaknefs their fubmitting to it would, in cafe of a fucceeding war, be but another word for the overthrow of their empire. It would depend on the naval force of the two empires on the Black fea, for which-ever fleet in cafe of a quarrel, was fuperior, they would nearly command the event of the war; if the Turks had the better, the Ruffians would be cut off from all the advantages propofed; and if victory declared for the latter, Conftantinople and all the provinces of the Ottoman empire would be expofed to them in the moft dangerous manner; and if the advantages of the Ruffians, in building and equipping fleets, with their territory behind them fo abounding with all

all sorts of materials, be considered, it can hardly be doubted but they would gain the most decisive superiority. Nor should I omit observing, that the mere possession of Azoph might be made a means of putting this plan in execution and carrying any future war, if well directed, to the gates of Constantinople.

Let any one consider the present aspect of affairs in that quarter, and the motions of the Russian troops, and it will be evident that this idea is now in being, and that, in all probability, before the present war sees a period, the Turks will find the arms of Russia infinitely heavier than in the last, and themselves attacked with a maritime force on the Black sea, much too great for them to contend with. I have been told, that it is a fixed determination of the Czarina's not to conclude this war without gaining a powerful establishment on the Black sea, so that Azoph may be but one step to connect with further and equally important acquisitions.

If we judge from the present state of the Russian army, we may look for great success; for the first foundation of it, experience, is strong in most of the officers, and the men may all be called veterans. It is the same army that saw all the campaigns against the king of Prus-

Pruſſia, that were beat without flying at Zorndorf, and conquered at Cunnerſdorf; and that have ſince been in continual action in Poland, and always victorious. It conſiſts of two hundred and fifty thouſand old ſoldiers, ſixty thouſand of which are horſe, better mounted, and finer troops, than any that were ever in the Ruſſian army before; with a train of artillery as fine as any in the world, and, what is of yet greater conſequence, well ſupplied with officers and engineers from all parts of Europe, attracted by every munificent encouragement. The Ruſſians are very ſenſible, that the loſſes they ſuſtained, and their want of ſucceſs is general, againſt the king of Pruſſia, was owing to their artillery being very badly ſerved, and it has given them a great eagerneſs to remedy this fatal evil; and at preſent I believe they have done it effectually; they will not any where be wanting in ſucceſs on that account.

This empire has not any neighbours to whom it is not much ſuperior in force, and in the conſtitution of its army. Poland is at its mercy, and will continue ſo till ſhe is reduced to a province, an event I ſhould never be much ſurprized at. Pruſſia is not comparable in power to Ruſſia, and could never make the ſtand againſt her arms again that we ſaw

in

in the last war; because the Russian army is better, more numerous, and with an artillery that yields to none in Europe; and, at the same time with an advantage she never enjoyed before, Poland behind her, three fourths of it absolutely in her power, to winter in, instead of falling back to Russia, which was the case before. I dwell the more upon these particulars, because it appears very clearly to me, that the next general war will see these two powers again in opposition, and I conjecture with very different success.

The present state of the Russian navy promises also well to the empire; for it never saw so many hands employed in it since the time of Peter the Great to the present. New ships are every day launching at Petersburg, and all the old ones repairing with great expedition; a stout squadron is fitting out, of such a force, that one would think the Empress meant to awe the Baltick, while her army is employed against the Turks. She has many ship-carpenters on the Tanais, and will be extremely formidable on the Black sea. So that if ever Russia began a war with a good prospect of success, it is this against the Turks.

There are many English at Petersburg; besides several gentlemen in the British factory,

with

with whom I became acquainted on my firſt coming hither: there are ſo many, that I am convinced we have more people in the Ruſſian ſervice by ſea and land, as well as in many other departments, than is conjectured in England. They certainly meet with good encouragement, or they would not be tempted to leave their own country; and very politick it is of the Empreſs to avail herſelf ſo ſtrongly of the alliance ſhe has with us; for nothing can be of more importance to her than getting as many of our officers by ſea and land into her ſervice, as poſſible; men ſhe has in abundance, and men that will ſtand for ever to be ſhot at; but the deſarts of Ruſſia will not give her experienced officers, tho' her own wars have formed many under the tuition of foreigners. Our engineers are of infinite conſequence to her; and ſhe has great numbers of ſhip-carpenters from Britain, as well as officers and common ſeamen. There never was a period more favourable to ſuch deſigns, than the concluſion of the late war, in which we had employed a greater number of forces both by land and ſea, than we could poſſibly keep up in peace; ſo that very many of them might be ſuppoſed willing enough to enter into the ſervice of a power in alliance with us;

an

an opportunity invaluable to the Emprefs, and of which I am clear she made good ufe.

This caufe, with the conftant trade we carry on with Peterfburg, fills that city with Englifh, Scotch, and Irifh; but they make no great figure; which is very eafily accounted for. From what I have feen of the Ruffians, the character I had heard of them appears very juft; they are a ftrange people, that carry in all the lower claffes the marks of civility juft emerging from barbarity. They are obedient, and very patient; but have a morofenefs that feems as if it would never be tamed. The loweft among them live in conftant feverity, yet that does not feem to bow down their fpirits or activity, as flavery does in all other countries: they make nothing of hardfhips, and will bear in continuance what would deftroy in a fhort time other people of lefs robuft conftitutions. The higher claffes however fhow nothing of this. They appear in fome meafure like other people, which is the effect of luxury among them, that every where foftens and humanizes the people among whom it comes. It may be thought odd by thofe who have never been in Ruffia, that I fhould talk of luxury among the Mufcovites; but there is no court in Europe, in which (the fituation and other circumftances of the country

try confidered,) is more luxury; and particularly in the articles of drefs, equipage, fervants, and the table; which is including the moft devouring branches of it. I have been three times at court, which is what we commonly call very fplendid; the dreffes of every body are more expenfive than I have any where feen: all in gold and filver and jewels, but fcarcely any tafte; they have in their dreffes but one ambition, which is to be as rich as poffible, and to have a great change; but as to having an idea of tafte, and real elegance, even the nobility feem not to know what it is. They are ridiculoufly fhewy, the climate confidered, in their coaches and fledges, thinking, in every inftance of this fort, that their rank can only be manifefted by an enormous expence. In their tables alfo, they are in the fame ftile; profufe in every thing: this has a very bad effect; for their revenues, a part of which ought to be expended upon their eftates in improvements, and finding employment for their neighbouring poor, are all fquandered in the luxury of the capital, giving employment to Englifhmen, Frenchmen and Dutchmen, inftead of their own countrymen. I know not what motive the government can have had for a long while in encouraging this profufion, unlefs it be to

keep

keep all the nobles poor, and thereby the more dependent.

The government of Russia is the most absolute in Europe; there is not even the appearance of the least barrier between the will of the sovereign and the people: all ranks are equally slaves to the Empress, not subjects; and their punishments shew the spirit of the legislature; the greatest nobility are liable to suffer the knout, that is, to be whipped to death; and other violent punishments are used, such as cutting out tongues, hanging up by the ribs, and many other efforts of barbarity, which shew the cruelty of despotism, without having any good effect. In the same spirit also we have seen the revolutions of the government: scarcely a sovereign dies a natural death, but is cut off; and, by a revolution in the government, a wife, a brother, or a sister, fixed in the throne; and all this performed by the regiments of guards, who, in fact, are pretorian cohorts, giving away the empire at their pleasure. This is ever a mark of a despotic government, which is always insecure in proportion to its severity.

It is amazing that politick princes, who are advanced to a throne by the favour of two or three regiments of guards, do not see in a clearer manner, that the same power which

gives

gives can take away; and, the moment they are firmly fixed in their power, do not extirpate the corps to whom they owe their advancement. Peter the Great faw the tendency of the Strelites and disbanded them, instituting three regiments of guards in their place; but thefe guards, from not being sent to diftant campaigns, and being conftantly around the perfon of the fovereign, are in fact the fame in power and opportunity as the Strelites. In a free government, or even in an abfolute monarchy, provided there is a shew of fome liberty, fuch as is in the kingdoms of France, Spain, &c. we do not fee the guards daring to act in this manner : but in countries of pure defpotifm, like Ruffia, Turkey, Perfia, &c. a prince, in order to be fafe, fhould have no guards in particular, but all the regiments of his army guards by turns; and when he is away from the capital, the garrifon of every place he is in, his guard for the time he is there. This method, tho' it might not infure them from all the evils which attend defpotifm, yet it would give them a much greater degree of fecurity than they could poffibly be in otherwife; which one would apprehend an object of the firft importance.

The Roman hiftory is full of inftances of
emperors

emperors being expofed, and others fet up by the Pretorian cohorts. Many are the Ottoman emperors who have been ftrangled by the Janiffaries; and the hiftories of other countries, under fimilar circumftances, abound with the like examples; which fhould make thofe monarchs, that owe their advancement to a few regiments felected from the reft of the army, throw all their forces upon the fame footing.

Peterfburg is tolerably gay, befides the brilliancy it derives from the court. There are a great many concerts, in which we find numerous performers of great merit, but all Germans; here are plays alfo exhibited but irregularly, and not with agreeable circumftances; an opera was eftablifhed, but it did not laft long; but by the accounts I have had, the gala time is when parties can be made on the ice: In winter all the country is covered with fnow, frozen fo hard, that that is the common feafon for travelling; and then innumerable parties are made in fledges, which are drawn on the frozen fnow over lakes, plains, rivers, bogs, &c. and muft form a fpectacle really aftonifhing to thofe who never beheld it: I am alfo told, that this way of travelling is fo very commodious, expeditious and agreeable, that a thoufand miles are paffed with much

much greater eafe than an hundred at any other feafon. As I purpofe feeing the fouthern provinces of the empire, I fhall therefore be gone before this entertainment is to be reaped; but, if I can make it tolerably convenient, will take a fhare in it on my return for Poland; tho' I have no great idea of travelling on fnow with any degree of information, or even much entertainment; for the foil, and the cultivation of it, and the ftate of the peafants, which afford me not only inftruction but entertainment, are then rendered invifible; fo that a journey full of the greateft variety muft have then an entire famenefs. This frozen fnow is, however, of prodigious confequence to the trade of this country; for carriage upon it is wonderfully cheap, and more expeditious than can well be conceived, which is a matter of great advantage to a country that has fuch roads as Ruffia.

The journey from Peterfburg to Pekin is the longeft that is gone by land throughout the world; it is near a year and half going, and as much returning, but then it is a trading carravan, much encumbered with baggage and merchandize, and in a part of the route with water; for all the men and cattle for many days are paffing fandy defarts, which are utterly void of water. Part of this immense route is performed on the snow, through a northerly part of Siberia, where there are no roads which are passable except on the snow. Of this vast journey, Mr. Bell in his travels has given a very good account. It is much owing to that gentleman, that the world knows any thing of Siberia, which is certainly one of the most extensive countries in the world; and, to the surprize of the western part of Europe, consists of several provinces, all of them three or four times as big as Great Britain, with a most fertile soil, and a mild climate in the southern parts, capable of feeding a most numerous population; but instead of being peopled in any proportion to its size, it is comparatively speaking a mere desart. But I can never be persuaded, that it is impossible for a sovereign of Russia, who sets heartily about it with judgment, activity, and penetration, to people all his dominions; or at least to put them in a way of doubling their numbers, in as short a period as ever our American colonies did, for this great work, a time of profound peace would be necessary, and an emperor that was of a truly philosophic disposition. Liberty must be diffused, all slavery of the lower ranks broken through, and every man allowed to become a farmer that pleases.

I purpoſed leaving Peterſburg the firſt week in September, being the furtheſt time I was informed that I could venture to ſet out upon a long journey, unleſs I ſtaid till the froſt and ſnow were ſet in : my deſign was to go to Moſcow, and from thence to Kiovia, the capital of the Ukraine, a country I was deſirous of ſeeing. Upon making enquiries into the proper preparations for ſuch a journey, I found there were but two plans; one to travel with a carravan to Moſcow, and the other to go only with my own attendants; of which I ſhould not have leſs than five, and all well armed : That it would not be adviſeable to travel with my own horſes, as I might procure a military order to be ſupplied by the peaſants, from poſt to poſt, at a ſmall price; and at the ſame time the owner of the horſes would attend as a guide. In purſuance of this advice I ſold my little Swediſh horſes, though ſomething againſt my will, and made up my guard with my own ſervant, my German poſtillion, and my Swede who underſtood the Ruſſian language, and to theſe I added by the favour of General Woroſoff (to whom I am otherwiſe much indebted) two foot ſoldiers from his own regiment. Theſe five fellows were each of them armed with a broad ſword, a pair of piſtols and a carbine; and I carried

carried a pair of piftols and a fhort rifled barrel gun, which were my arms from Denmark through all Sweden, though I never had any neceffity of ufing them. Thus equipped, I was affured I might travel in perfect fafety through all Ruffia.

CHAPTER V.

Journey from Peterfburg to Mofcow—Defcription of the Country—Great Settlement of Poles—Mofcow—Journey into The Ukraine—Account of that fine Province—Defcription of the Agriculture of it—Culture of Hemp, Tobacco, &c.

I LEFT Peterfburg the 6th of September, and with much difficulty got to Juamgorod, which is fifty miles, through a country which is alternately a marfh and woods. From thence to Novogorod took me three days, being the diftance of one hundred miles. I laid both nights at Ruffian inns. I travelled in the character of a general officer in the King of England's fervice, which was of no flight ufe to me; for it is not eafy to conceive the refpect which all the lower ranks of people pay to the military, of whatever nation, provided they make any figure; and the number

ber of my attendants, with their being so well armed, and the various languages we spoke, seemed to imprefs the people with a notion that I was a perfon of very great confequence. The Ruffians have nothing in them that one can properly call civility, but I met with the moſt perfect obſequiouſnefs and obedience; and having provided myſelf with good bread, I lived upon excellent fiſh throughout the journey. About Novogorod the country is part of it cultivated, but the incloſures are thin, and there do not ſeem to be any great exertions of induſtry in it, but the ſoil appears to be a fine, deep, rich loam.

September the 11th, I got to Midna, which is above forty miles. This line of country is beautiful, being in fine but gentle inequalities, and only ſprinkled with ſmall woods, and well watered with rivers: there is much cultivated land; but the harveſt was all got in. I ſaw ſome crops of turneps, ſuch as are common in Sweden, and as fine, but the people ſeem to be very miſerable. Many of the peaſants have farms, but then they can only work them when their landlords allow: three or four days in the week they labour on the lands of their maſters, finding ſometimes cattle and implements, in conſideration of being allowed the reſt of their time on their own farms; yet for thefe they pay a confiderable rent in products, and are befides open to the fupplying all military travellers with horfes, for which they get a very fpare allowance, and fometimes nothing at all. In a word, their ftate is fo little better than the common labourers, who work conftantly for their lords, that I did not find it a matter of envy to the latter.

The 12th I reached Thedray, a little town, prettily fituated near a river, the fame country continuing for forty-four miles, and much of it tolerably well cultivated. I paffed through feveral very extenfive plains of meadow, that appeared very fine, but were not well ftocked with cattle. The villages feem very well peopled.

The 14th I got to Twera, which is a confiderable town on the river Wolga, the diftance above eighty miles. The peafants have hitherto furnifhed me very well with horfes; yet their pay is not three farthings a mile, with fomething for the peafant. I have given to the value of four-pence Englifh for a day's journey, with which they feem to be very well fatisfied; from whence I conjecture that they ufually have nothing. This line of country is pretty well peopled. I paffed through feveral towns, and many villages, with

with some cultivated country that was cut into inclosures, and appeared to be kept in good order. Upon making enquiry, they informed me, that they cultivated barley, oats, and buck-wheat; and, from the best conjecture I can make from the intelligence they gave me, in Russian weight and measure, to the amount of between two and three quarters English per acre. All the lands that are in culture here belong to the nobility, whose agents manage them with the peasants. But some they pointed out at a distance, that belonged to others, who I found were possessors of the land, but not nobles; in other words, gentlemen. It was with some difficulty that I could get my two soldiers to behave with any decency to the peasants; they were always ready for giving them a blow, when gentle words would do to the full as well; but I curbed this licentiousness, which gave me a clear idea of the government of Russia, and at the same time convinced me, that all the Empress's fine schemes for encouraging agriculture must inevitably come to nothing. The peasant who conducted me to Twera told me, on the road, that such a track of land was his father's farm; that it belonged to him, not being hired of any landlord; and would, after his father's death, come to him.

I said, then he would have an opportunity of living much better, and being more comfortable than at present. He replied, no; that if he got any thing, the Count Woronoſkoy would take it, for there was a payment (which I took to be in the nature of a quit-rent) to him out of it. I obſerved ſeveral good tracks that were arable; he ſaid that his father's land was chiefly meadow, but he hired ſome ploughed ground of the Count; and I found that the rent of good arable land was two ſhillings an acre, that was in regular culture. But this is not a mark of great cheapneſs, the prices of all products being proportionate; for good bread is, through this country, at about a farthing a pound, and mutton and beef ſomething better than three farthings, but under a penny; ſo that every thing elſe muſt of courſe be proportionate. And a farmer muſt cultivate a large track of ground to raiſe a ſmall ſum of money; but the caſe is, that money is ſo valuable, that they raiſe no more products than neceſſary for their common purchaſes and rent, and the ſmall ſum they bring anſwers where all things are proportioned. I found from this man's account, that a farmer, who lived upon his own eſtate, was at the mercy of the neareſt nobleman, and, if he grew rich, would ſurely

be

be fleeced by him. It is impoffible to introduce improvements into fuch a country without an entire new fyftem.

As I advanced in my journey, I every where made enquiries after new fettlements on the lands belonging to the Emprefs; but heard nothing of them till I got to Twera : there they told me, that in the foreft of Volkoufkile, about an hundred miles to the fouth-weft, was a very large new colony of Poles, fettled at the expence of the Czarina. I immediately determined to go out of my way to view it, that I might have an opportunity to fee in what manner they were fixed, and what a reception they met with. I got there the 16th, paffing through a country, the chief of which is wafte, being either foreft or meadow, but with few villages. I found the fettlement of Poles confifted of about fix hundred families; and pleafed me better than any thing I had feen in Ruffia. Each family has a fmall, but not a bad houfe, built of wood, and covered with fhingles; a houfe as good or better than the generality of fmall farm-houfes in England, where the mud walls would give foreigners an idea that we were the pooreft nation in Europe. Behind every houfe was an inclofure of about fifty Englifh acres in one field. The fence was a ditch

ditch and parapet, with a row of young plants for a hedge, that seemed to be a kind of elm. Each inclosure came down to a rivulet, where cattle might water. Each family had two sheep, and a ram, to a certain number, a cow, and a couple of oxen to till the arable, with a cart and a plough; all which were at the Empress's expence, and do not cost what they would in England. This may be conceived, when I give the rates. Two oxen for ploughing and carting come to but five pounds; a cow to thirty shillings; a sheep eighteen-pence; a plough four shillings; a cart nine shillings; each house cost the Empress about four and twenty shillings; and every family had an allowance of provision the first year from the neighbouring country, which cost her nothing; so that the total expence, per family, was only eight pounds ten shillings; and many of the families consist of eight or nine persons. The farms were all under culture, and subdivided by the people themselves; and I observed that these inner fences were done exactly in the same manner as the surrounding ones. Some had four fields, others five, and some six. The land, when they settled it, was waste forest, but not many trees on it, that yielded a wild and luxuriant grass: it is a red loam on clay. The peasants cultivate wheat without exception, which they had been used to in Poland; each had one field of it; also a crop of barley, oats, or rice; with a piece of beans, and another of turneps. Their farms were in general in good order, and they seemed to be extremely diligent and industrious in their management. Some of them had vastly increased their cattle, keeping as many as they pleased on the adjoining forest: some had more than twenty sheep, ten cows, and six oxen; but they had greatly increased their farms, which the Emprefs allows, provided the former portion is all in culture. They all seemed to be perfectly happy, being entirely free from all oppression by being on the lands of the crown; and there is no doubt but they will in time yield a fine revenue, without any severity being employed.

Some of them had pieces of hemp, which thrives with them so well, that its culture increases among them daily. I enquired particularly into the value of an acre, and found that it was worth upon the spot from fifty shillings to four pounds, which I think is very considerable, and shews that these new colonies may prove a source of very great wealth and population.

It

It is extremely evident from this inſtance, that the way of bringing improvements to bear in Ruſſia, is not by encouragements given to the peaſants, unleſs they could at once be ſet as free as in other countries, which I am convinced already is an impoſſibility, from what I have ſeen on this journey; becauſe the nobility and other land-owners, to whom they are vaſſals, fleece and oppreſs them to ſuch a degree, that they can never be ſecure of any property, unleſs their encouragement comes from their own lords. Even they who are not vaſſals, but have poſſeſſions of their own, are trampled on by the ſoldiery. No improvement, by giving them a greater degree of liberty, can therefore have any effect, unleſs it comes from their lords; as in this caſe of the Poliſh emigrants. The Empreſs fixing them upon the crown-lands, they are vaſſals of the crown, and all the liberty ſhe chuſes to give them they will ſecurely enjoy, without any one's daring to injure them in any reſpect; and as the ſovereign can never profitably cultivate an extenſive domain for her own account, this is the only means of working improvements; and they cannot fail of proving moſt highly profitable.

And the nobility have it alſo in their power to make the ſame improvements upon their own

own eftates, becaufe under their protection the peafants would be fecure. But as to all general improvements in hufbandry, it is merely impoffible that they fhould be attended with the leaft effect. Every landlord has every thing in his power upon his own lands, provided, I mean, he be of rank and confequence; and they have the ability, by means of the flavery of their peafants, to work very great effects, if they pleafed to undertake them. Laws or edicts therefore muft be directed to them: the rewards for a proper conduct fhould all be granted to them; the Emprefs fhould addrefs herfelf to them, and let them find favour at court in proportion to the cultivation of their eftates: thefe are the only means of doing great things.

The crown lands are fo amazingly extenfive, that very great things might in this manner be done, and far more effectually than by general laws, in a country where the people are fo habituated to flavery, that it would be a vain attempt to free them under all mafters. Thefe fix hundred families had at once thirty thoufand acres in culture, befides the increafe, which by many of them was very confiderable; all which will, in procefs of time, yield a great revenue to the crown, befides the acquifition of ftrength

which

which the empire receives by the addition of population, and the amount of so much industry as all these people create. After five years this colony is to pay an annual rent, which in ten more will be increased, and after that remain a freehold to the Poles, subject only to that rent. An idea of the field which the Empress has for improvement may be conjectured by one contiguous track of waste and forest, partly in the Ziranni province, which contains above thirty-seven millions of English acres, and belongs to the crown, besides tracks in Siberia and Tartary ten times as large. It is therefore extremely evident, that the great object of Russian politicks should be the peopling and cultivating the crown lands; which, if managed with unremitted diligence, and without sparing expence, might be continually on the improvement, and in such swift manner, that the quantity of land rendered profitable might soon be immensely great.

This colony of Poles have a market in the middle of their settlement on the great road, where merchants resort to buy their spare products, hemp, &c. bringing all those sorts of commodities which they want; and this trade occasions a circulation among them which is highly advantageous. The report of the indulgence and benefits they have met with has had great effect in Poland; so that they pointed out to me a track of land contiguous, where they soon expected two hundred families more. Having viewed several farms of the settlers and made such enquiries as I thought necessary, I set out for Moscow without returning to Twera: the distance is one hundred and seventeen miles; and I arrived there the 20th, passing through a very finely variegated country, well watered and wooded, and spread in fine plains, with many villages scattered through them; and much appearance of cultivation: all this country is in the hands of three or four nobles, whose stewards direct the management of it.

This city is the greatest in the empire; it was once strongly fortified for this part of the world, but the security of the present times has made every thing unnecessary except a wall: It is about sixteen miles in circumference, and contains about half a million of inhabitants, till lately the Czars spent a part of the year here; but the palace, which is a very indifferent one, having been damaged by fire, they have not of late years been there; but notwithstanding this, Moscow is the residence of a vast number of the nobility, indeed of three fourths of those whose offices

or

or expectations do not oblige them to attend the court; in which instance there is a greater appearance of liberty than in most other countries; for in general, all the nobility of a kingdom flock to the seat of government.

Moscow is very irregularly built; but it is a beautiful city, from the windings of the river, and from many eminences which are covered with groves of fine tall trees, and from numerous gardens, and lawns, which opening to the water give it a most pleasing airy appearance. I expected to see nothing but wooden houses, but was agreeably surprized at the sight of many very fine fabricks of brick and stone. It is beyond comparison a finer city than Petersburg. The number of churches and chapels, amounting it is said to eighteen hundred, make a great figure in the printed descriptions of this city; but from the appearance of them I should suppose the fact false, and that out of great numbers very few are worthy of note. I saw the great bell, which is the largest in the world, and indeed a most stupendous thing it is. They have many other bells in the city, which much exceed any thing that is elsewhere to be met with; the Russians being remarkably fond of this ornament of their churches.

There

There is a very confiderable manufacture at Mofcow of various hemp fabricks; particularly, fail cloth and fheeting, which employs fome thoufands of looms, and many thoufands of people; the hemp is moſt of it brought from the Ukraine: there are alſo great numbers of confiderable merchants here, who carry on a very extenfive commerce with all parts of the empire; for there is water carriage from hence to the Black and Cafpian feas, and with but few interruptions to the Baltick alfo, which are circumftances that make it the center of a very great commerce.

This city is much better fituated for the metropolis of the empire than Peterfburg: It is almoſt in the center of the moſt cultivated parts of it; communicating in the manner above-mentioned with the three inland feas, not at a great diſtance from the moſt important province of the empire, the Ukraine; open to the fouthern territories on the Black fea, and by means of the rivers Wolga and the Don commanding an inland navigation of prodigious extent. Its vicinity alfo to the countries, which muſt always be the feat of any wars with the Turks, the enemies moſt to be attended to of all thofe with whom the Ruffians wage war; upon the whole made it infinitely a better fituation for the feat of government,

vernment, than that of Peterſburg, which is at the very extremity of the empire, and poſſeſſing few of theſe advantages. Founding that city, and making it the feat of foreign commerce and naval power, was an admirable exertion of genius; but the ſeat of government ſhould always have been at Moſcow.

The 23d I left that city, taking the road towards Ukraine—I was fortunate in having very fine clear weather, and found the roads every where exceedingly good, no autumnal rains having yet fallen. I got that night to Molaſky, the diſtance about ſixty miles, nor did I find ſuch a day's journey too much for the horſes; the country all this way is a level plain, very fertile, and much of it well cultivated, with many villages, and in general, a well peopled territory: the peaſants ſeemed tolerably eaſy, but ſcarcely any of them have any property. From Molaſky, fifty ſix miles carried me the next day to Arcroiſy, a ſmall town; ſituated in a territory not ſo well-peopled as the preceding; the villages thinner, and but little of the ſoil cultivated, being covered with much timber of great ſize and beauty. The 25th I reached Demetriovitz, at the diſtance of more than fifty miles, every ſtep of which was acroſs a foreſt in which I ſaw not the leaſt veſtige of any habitation: the road was not difficult to find, even if I had not had a guide, but it is not much frequented; the mercantile people making this part of the journey to the Ukraine by water: This immenfe track of wild country, is part open meadow and part covered with timber, which would in England be thought a glorious fight: the foil is all a fine fand, and, if I may judge from the fpontaneous vegetation, a moft fertile loam; fo that nothing is wanting but an induftrious population: but without that, the whole territory is of little worth. I baited the horfes in the middle of the foreft, and refrefhed myfelf and company, much admiring the uncommon extent of country that was without the leaft appearance of being inhabited: I apprehended that the country muft have a great refemblance of the boundlefs plains and woods of Louifiana.

The 26th I rode forty miles through an uninhabited plain to Serenfky; no timber in it, but all one level fertile meadow. I faw fome herds of cattle feeding as if wild, but the land was not a tenth part ftocked; for the grafs, if we turned out of the road, was up almoft to the bellies of the horfes; fuch meadow would, I apprehend, in any part of England let readily for five and twenty fhillings an acre, yet here of no value: fuch are the effects of population, liberty, and induftry!

The same distance the 27th. carried me to Brensky, a pretty little town on the banks of a river in the middle of a forest; a place truly romantick. I felt myself rather fatigued with hard riding since I left Petersburg, and therefore rested myself here the 28th, lest a continuance of this great exercise should give me a fit of illness, for which Russia is the most unfit place in the world; for every man out of Petersburg and Moscow must be his own physician.

The 29th I got to Staradoff at the distance of fifty miles: full twenty of which are through a rich and pleasant country, much of it very well cultivated; they were getting in part of their harvest: they cultivate all the grain and pulse common in England; and from what I saw I have little doubt but their husbandry is extremely good. They generally manage their lands in the system of sowing first hemp, then oats, then turneps, then wheat or rye, but much of the former is sown: after this husbandry of five years which is sometimes varied to six or seven two crops of hemp being taken they leave the land fallow for three four or five years; by fallow is not however meant ploughing it all that time, but letting it run to grass and weeds; it is presently covered thickly; the second year all the weeds disappear,

disappear, and they have a very fine meadow, without the trouble of sowing any hay seeds, which they keep as the feeding ground of their farms for several years, as their cattle require; and whenever they plough it up again they are sure to find a field entirely fertilized and ready to yield abundant crops. I should have apprehended that this management would have filled the land with the seeds of weeds, which, upon breaking it up, would have destroyed their crop; but an agent that seemed to belong to some man of a large estate answered me by saying that the first crop they sowed, being hemp, entirely cleaned the ground for all the successive ones; that in case the effect was not perfected, a second would infallibly do it; for I found they had an idea here, that hemp is a great cleaner of the land, and that no weeds can live among it; which is what I do not recollect any writer of husbandry mentions, as being the practice of English farmers. It is one instance, among many others I have met with, in which I regret not making myself better acquainted with the husbandry of England, before I made enquiries into that of other countries. The quantity of hemp sown in all this country is very confiderable; indeed I was told, that this province, which joins a part of the Ukraine in some

some places, is much like that country, only the soil not quite so fine. The land here is a rich loam, wet, and much inclinable to a clay. They reckon an acre of hemp, one year with another, to be worth three pounds; an acre of wheat yields three quarters, and as much of rye; four quarters of barley, and as much or more of oats. They have fine crops of beans about five quarters upon an acre. They do not cultivate so many turneps as they should, but trust many of their cattle all winter long on the waste, where they find herbage enough, notwithstanding the snow, to keep them alive: but it would certainly be much better husbandry to keep them better, and collect their dung. They have large herds, which in summer are kept in fine order by means of the exceeding good pasturage, which all the meadows yield in vast plenty. All this country belongs to different noblemen, and is cultivated by their stewards and agents, who seem to know their business very well; but the peasants seem to be very poor, having scarcely any signs of cultivation around their cottages, and yet they are fed by what they raise for themselves on certain days. I remark, that the peasants in this empire are in general happy in proportion to the neglect under which the country lies; in the midst of vast wastes and forests

rests they seem to be tolerably easy; but any tracks well cultivated, are done at their expence, and they appear very near on the same rank, as the blacks in our sugar colonies.

From Staradoff to Czernicheu is seventy five miles, which I rode in two days, arriving there the 1st of November. Part of this track is as well cultivated as that on the other side of Staradoff, but much of it is covered with forest. I observed hemp in many of the fields, and some of it was not yet pulled, though the harvest was generally in. Czernicheu is a very well built town, finely situated on the banks of the river Desna, which is navigable for barges of fifty tons, is very well fortified, and inhabited by about fifteen thousand people; many of whom carry on a considerable trade with Kiovia, and, by the Nieper, with Poland. All the track of country, which lies upon the river Desna, is very rich, and well cultivated. Many of the inhabitants of Czernicheu are Cossack Tartars; but a traveller has no more reason to fear them, than the inhabitants of any other part of Russia; for the government, although milder in the Ukraine, and the neighbouring provinces, from having been conquered from Poland, is yet the same, and the police as strict as in any other part of the empire. I made enquiries here concerning the danger of travelling through the Ukraine in this time of war; and they aſſured me, that whether it was war or peace, I ſhould not ſee the leaſt appearance of any danger; that I ſhould find the Ukraine, tho' inhabited by Tartars, as well a regulated province as any county in England. They ſaid, there had been no incurſions made into any of theſe provinces, as the theatre of the war was puſhed on to the countries around the Black ſea, and where they doubted not but it would continue.

November the 3d I reached Kiovia, the capital of the Ukraine, and fourſcore miles from Czernicheu. The road leads on the banks of the Deſna, through a beautiful country; great part of it being well-peopled and cultivated. It is inhabited by Tartarian deſcendants; but I found the preſent Coſſacks, who have very little idea of huſbandry, come far from the eaſtward, from countries that reach to the river Don, at the diſtance of above a thouſand miles from hence. The preſent race of the Ukraine are a civilized people, and the beſt husbandmen in the Ruſſian empire.

Kiovia, one of the moſt conſiderable cities I have ſeen in Ruſſia, is a place well known in the

the hiftory of that empire; for tho' it has been fubject to many revolutions, which reduced it to a low ftate compared with its former grandeur, yet it has now recovered all thofe antient blows; it is well built of brick and ftone: the ftreets are wide and ftrait, and well paved; it has a very noble cathedral, much of it lately rebuilt, and eleven other churches. It has forty thoufand inhabitants; and is ftrongly fortified. The Nieper is here a noble river; and feveral larger rivers falling into it, after wafhing fome of the richeft provinces of Poland, enable this town to carry on a very confiderable commerce. It is the grand magazine of all the commodities of the Ukraine, particularly hemp and flax, which in this fine province are raifed in greater quantities, and of a better quality, than in any other part of Europe. The Ukraine is the richeft province in the Ruffian empire. Part of it formerly was a province of Poland, and the reft an independent fovereignty, under a Tartar prince; but the whole is now a mere province of Ruffia, and much the richeft acquifition that crown has made. It is upon an average two hundred and fifty miles long eaft to weft; and one hundred and forty broad north to fouth.

November

November 5th, I left the capital of this province; and as I purpofed making a circular detour of the weftern part, I went to Buda that day, which is about fifty miles; moft of the country rich and very well cultivated; the foil is a black loam, and they raife in it the various forts of grain and pulfe that are commonly met with in England. I paffed through great tracks of ftubble ground, from off which the wheat, barley, and oats were carried. And I obferved numerous hemp grounds, though not fo much of the country is under that crop as corn; in fome villages where I made enquiries, they fpoke nothing but the Polifh language, and of a dialect which my interpreter for the Ruffian knew nothing of, though he had affured me he underftood Polifh very well; but I met with other peafants who fpoke Ruffian, and they informed me that their products of hemp arofe in value fometimes to fix pounds an acre, but three or four pounds were a common crop; of wheat four quarters; barley five, and oats and beans fix, and fometimes more an acre; which appeared to me to be all very confiderable quantities. Their grounds are moft of them inclofed with ditches, to fome of which are hedges, but not to all. They have fine meadow grounds, which they convert to hemp, in the manner I related above,

bove, but leave them under grafs for ten or twelve years before they break them up; and keep them in a tillage-management as long: upon some grounds they have three crops of hemp running. Flax they alfo cultivate, but they do not reckon it fo profitable as hemp. In the management of their cattle they are very good farmers: they have large ftocks, and they houfe them all whenever the fnow is above four inches deep upon the ground; they litter them down well with ftraw, and feed them with hay or turneps: cows are their principal ftock; and they fell immenfe quantities of butter and cheefe, though it is extremely remarkable, that not many years ago they knew not what butter was. The property of all this country is very much divided; here are very few great eftates belonging to nobility: the old inhabitants of the country were very free, and had a great equality among them; and this in poffeffions as well as other circumftances; and fortunately this continues, though in fubjection to Ruffia, moft of the peafants are little farmers, whofe farms are their own, with ten times the liberty among them that I any where elfe faw in Ruffia; the government are extremely cautious of oppreffing or offending them, for they never will be in want of

folicitations

solicitations from the Turks to join the Tartars in alliance with the Porte. They pay a considerable tribute, but raise it among themselves according to their own customs; and they also furnish the Russian armies with a great many very faithful troops. These points, with the immense value of the trade the Russians carry on by means of their products, hemp and flax in particular, render the province of the first importance. ' I passed in this line of fifty miles, great numbers of villages and scattered farms.

Buda is a little town, or rather a large village, prettily situated between two rivers in a country perfectly pleasant. I turned off to the north-west and got the 6th to Kordyne, a little town fifty two miles from Buda: All this country is equal to the preceding day's journey; I never saw a track of land that had more resemblance to the best parts of England. Nothing could be more fortunate than the weather for my expedition; the rains usually come very heavy the middle of September, and soon after them frosts and snow, but I have yet had a constant azure sky, with warm winds. If it holds five days more, I shall have passed this province, and I do not hear that there is any thing worthy of notice between the Ukraine and Petersburg, therefore

fore the weather will not be fo eſſential to the journey. I remarked in the country I paſſed to day, ſeveral tobacco plantations; they reſemble hop grounds when the hillocks are not poled; they reckon it as profitable as hemp, which is owing I believe to the ready vent they find for all they cultivate; the Tartars upon the Black ſea, and the Kalmucks buy large quantities; and they are not ſo nice in the ſeparation of the ſorts, as our planters in Virginia are obliged to be, though they ſell their product for as good a price; but I do not think there grows the leſs hemp on account of their tobacco; it ſeems to be cultivated, inſtead of ſowing quite ſo much corn as in other parts; an acre of tobacco is worth five pounds in a good year. They have large houſes highly run up for drying it. They think the land cannot be too rich for either hemp or tobacco, and accordingly plant them on freſh land.

The 7th I reached Leſzozyn, at the diſtance of ſix and thirty miles, the country continuing the ſame; much hemp and tobacco being planted through the whole: At a village by the way where I ſtopped to make enquiries, I found they preferred a red clay for their hemp, and planted all the black mold with tobacco. I obſerved many ploughs

at

at work, some with six horses, of a little weak breed, but in general each was drawn by four stout oxen. They were turning up wheat stubbles, and said they ploughed them before winter, that the frosts and snow might improve the ground, which seems to be good management. I think I never saw such deep ploughing as these peasants give their ground: I measured nine inches perpendicular after a plough drawn by four oxen; what the depth is in England I never noticed particularly, but believe it is not so much as this. Their ploughs are very well constructed; if I may judge by their entirely turning over the land, they are all of iron, having no wood about them; a sort I had never seen till I came into the Ukraine; nor have they any wheels which our plough-wrights in England think so essential. I remarked here several very noble crops of cabbages, and in such vast quantities, that I concluded they must feed their cattle with them, and was right in the conjecture: they used formerly to cultivate only the Swedish turnep for this purpose, but cabbages (they are a red sort, and come to a monstrous size, 25 or 30 lb. for instance) by degrees have come into fashion among them, so as to be the crop on which they entirely depend, with help of hay for the winter sustenance of their cattle. They
sow

sow the seed early in the spring, and plant them when of a proper size, into the field in rows, and afterwards keep them as clean as they do their tobacco, by constant hoeing: an acre of them will winter four or five large oxen; they reckon the culture extremely profitable. They have also whole fields of potatoes, some for their own use, and some for sale, there being a great demand for them at Ockzacow, on the Black sea, whither they are sent by water; but I cannot help thinking they must have a sort unknown in England: I rode into a field where a crop was taking up, and great numbers were as large as the body of a quart bottle; I never saw such before. They freely gave me a few of these large ones to take away for seed; they are planted by slices in the same manner as ours: the peasants here think that lands of moderate fertility do for them. Such a potatoe, I should apprehend, might, for feeding cattle, be made of very great advantage to the husbandry of England; they yield from twelve to fifteen hundred bushels per acre.

The 8th I rode to Kwafowa, a large village, the distance about forty miles. This country is, in some places, a continued level plain; in others it is variegated with gentle hills, which never rise into moun-

mountains, but are cultivated to the tops: Hemp and tobacco are common crops through the whole, and also some flax, but not in equal quantities. All the country is divided into small estates, or rather farms, cultivated by the owners; though I am told that in some parts of the province to the south, where I have not been, there are large estates belonging to the nobles, and that those parts are not near so well peopled or cultivated as these parts; which is a strong proof that much of the good husbandry met with in the Ukraine is owing to the peasants being owners of their lands, and vassalage almost unknown in the province. It cannot be doubted but the Empress may bring the crown lands of Russia, on all the frontier of Poland, into as flourishing a state as parts of this province, if she encourages foreign settlers with all the spirit she has hitherto shewn, since it is in her power to give them all the advantages which the inhabitants of the Ukraine enjoy. They have, it is true, a noble country, equal, I think, in soil, &c. to Flanders, and almost as well cultivated; but I have seen in other provinces of this empire immense waste tracks of land, not at all inferior in every thing derived from nature; but enslaved peasants are utterly inconsistent with a flourishing husbandry.

The

The 9th I got to Norodiza, the diftance forty miles: the foil in this track is inferior to what I have paffed; but the people appear to be excellent hufbandmen: they have fome hemp, but little tobacco, only a plantation here and there. I paffed through feveral villages, which have been lately built by fugitive Poles, who have fixed themfelves here on fome fmall waftes, by leave of the government, but without any expence. The 10th I had a very hard day's journey to Belechoka, the diftance more than fixty miles, and the road in fome places marfhy. Only parts of this track are well cultivated, but no hemp, flax, or tobacco are raifed; there are alfo fome waftes, but they will not be fuch long, for the Poles are planting themfelves on them very faft. Here I paffed out of the province of Ukraine.

It is this territory which raifes nineteenths of the hemp and flax which we import at fuch a vaft expence from Ruffia; it is therefore deferving of a little attention; for the beft politicians, who have given moft attention to the affairs of our American colonies, have all of them infifted very ftrenuoufly upon the poffibility and even eafe of fupplying ourfelves totally from thence. What truth there is in this I know not; but it will be of ufe to confider this province of the Ukraine with more attention than any writer has hitherto done, becaufe from knowing it perfectly we may judge how far we can reafon by analogy when America is fpoken of; and this is the more neceffary, as the accounts which have hitherto been publifhed of it are ftrangely contradictory; for on one hand they tell us truly, that the Ruffian hemp comes from thence; but on the other, they give fuch a picture of the ftate of the country, that one would fuppofe it poffeffed by herds of wandering Coffacks, which is utterly inconfiftent with the idea of fuch a ftate of agriculture as is neceffary for making fo great a proficiency in the culture of hemp and flax. All thefe accounts muft have been copied one from another, and the firft of them at leaft a century and half old. To be convinced of which, let any perfon look into the account of the Ukraine, in that very judicious collection of voyages and travels, entitled *Harris*'s; there he will meet with mention indeed of the great fertility of the country, but three-fourths of the particulars given are relative to its wandering Tartar inhabitants; and the words hemp or flax never once ufed; and a defcription of the people given that would be utterly inconfiftent with fuch agriculture; and this is the cafe with all the books that I have

turned

turned to; but the reason must be, the country's being so extremely out of the way of all travellers, that not a person in a century goes to it, who takes notes of his observations with intention to lay them before the world: very few such go even to Petersburg; now and then one crosses Russia towards Persia; but all keep a thousand or two of miles from the Ukraine; and hence it is that the greatest changes happen in such remote parts of the world, without any thing of the matter being known. And our writers of geography, who are every day publishing, copy each other in so slavish a manner, that a fact in 1578 is handed down to us as the only information we can have in 1769; a circumstance which reigns in all the books of general geography that I have seen. Let me here add, that I have, in travelling to gain information, visited those countries about which it would be in vain to consult books; for, Holland and Flanders alone excepted, all the rest of the present journey is through countries, the former accounts of which are entirely false, not from errors in the authors, but from great changes that have happened in a long course of years. But to return.

It has been supposed that hemp and flax, coming to us from so northern a place as Pe- tersburg,

tersburg, would grow in the midst of perpetual frosts and snows; but though we import it from latitude 60, yet it all grows in the Ukraine, which lies between latitude 47 and 52, and is besides as fine, mild a climate as any in Europe: this is the latitude of the south of France; and with these advantages, the soil is superior to most I have seen, being in general a very rich, deep mould, between a loam and a dry clay, but without any of that tenacious stickiness which is so disagreeable in moving through a clay country in England. I am clear in the importance of conveying a precise idea, when we speak of soils; but not having been used to practical husbandry so much as I wish I had, I cannot properly make use of the necessary technical terms. To these advantages, which this province enjoys, I should certainly add, whether from accident or natural ingenuity, their good husbandry, which is much superior to any thing that I have seen since I left Flanders.

After giving these particulars, we may examine, upon a good foundation, the capability of our colonies affording hemp and flax in equal quantities. Those gentlemen who have travelled through them, best know how well they answer to the above description: but if I may be permitted to speak on the authorities which

which many modern relations give us, the settlements on the sea-coasts of North-America will never yield hemp in any quantities; the climate is much too changeable and severe; sharp cutting frosts are met with in Carolina, in 30 degrees of latitude, and a burning sun, equal in heat to any part of the world: in New-England, Nova-Scotia, &c. where hemp has been attempted, it has always failed, from the severity of the climate, and the badness of the lands. But all accounts give a very contrary description of the countries on the Mississippi: from the descriptions which I have read of the track on that river, from lat. 33 to lat. 40, I should apprehend it to be, of all other places in America, the most adapted to this culture: for the soil is rich, black, and very deep; the climate much more regular and pleasant than on the sea-coast, which is all marshes and swamps, and the lands in immense plenty, and all fresh. Hemp certainly might be raised in those parts to great advantage, provided the descriptions of them, which we have had, are just; which I do not see any reason to doubt. But then the misfortune is, that these beautiful tracks of country are without inhabitants; and great numbers of people are necessary for an advantageous culture of hemp. Another circumstance

stance to be considered is, the profit of such an application of the land: hemp would never be cultivated to any purpose in Carolina, or our southern colonies, if the climate was proper, because rice and indico, and I believe even cotton, pay the planter much superior profits; and if indico and cotton were introduced on the Mississippi, as in all probability they would be, hemp would be neglected till those markets failed which took off the more beneficial articles. But, on the other hand, we ought not to regret this, for the national profit is proportionably greater: the more the planter's advantage, the more the national income is increased. Hemp in fact is not an article of culture that is comparable to many others in profit, and will consequently never be cultivated except in those countries where corn and pulse, and other less profitable articles, would occupy the land if that did not; but when the soil and climate will do for richer commodities, it is idle to suppose that poorer ones will be attended to.

If, therefore, it is an essential point to raise all the hemp in our colonies which we bring from Russia, new plantations must be formed on the Mississippi, in a latitude that will not do for the rich American staples; such for instance as that of 37 to 40, or thereabouts.

The

The country so included is one of the finest in the world for all common husbandry; so that the inhabitants, like those of the Ukraine, would very easily raise all the necessaries of life, at the same time that their principal attention was given to hemp as their staple.

CHAPTER VI.

Journey to Petersburg through the Frontiers of Poland—Observations on the State of several Provinces — Russian Acquisitions—Remarks on the War between the Russians and the Turks—Journey to Archangel, and through Lapland—Return to Petersburg—Livonia.

NOVEMBER the 11th I left Belachoka, and rode to Rzeezyka, at the distance of forty-four miles, through a country very different from the Ukraine; for it consists of little besides marshes, with but few inhabitants. It is to be noted, that most of this track is in Poland, and Rzeezyka is the capital of a province once Polish, and which all the maps I have lay down as a part of Poland; but I am convinced there have been strange changes wrought by force of Russian arms on the frontiers of that kingdom. The town is large, populous, and strongly

strongly fortified; but as much Russian as Moscow. Here are great numbers of Poles, it is true; but all the houses which the war had emptied are filled up carefully with Russian families; and there is a Russian garrison, Russian government, and, in a word, scarcely any thing Polish in it. By this extreme political conduct, that empire makes very great acquisitions on the side of Poland, without the world knowing any thing of the matter; which is the effect of the miserable government, or rather anarchy, under which they live; and which is the pretence for the Russian troops swarming over the whole kingdom; so that three parts in four of it are a province of Russia, and probably the whole will in a little time, which may be more advantageous to the kingdom; for no despotism of the East is so great a curse to a people, as the furious military anarchy that reigns at present in Poland. I have received accounts from various people since I have been in Russia, from which I should apprehend, that full half the inhabitants of that great country have been cut off and starved within these ten years. Near half the kingdom is absolutely in the hands of the Russians, who receive pretty heavy taxes from it, and also recruits for their army against

the

the Turks: vast numbers of people are, by this means, also transported into Russia; for Polish noblemen, who declare against the Russian party, are driven entirely from their estates, and great numbers of their peasants removed immediately into Russia, with their cattle and all their effects; so that the Empress may easily have increased her subjects in the degree which I was told, at Petersburg. And it certainly must be allowed, that the cards she plays in this manner ensure her a game uncommonly advantageous. The poor Poles, driven about, and reduced to the utmost misery by their own people, must be very ready to fix upon lands in Russia, and be vassals only to the Empress. If this scene of confusion therefore lasts much longer in Poland, that kingdom will be entirely depopulated, and the Russian provinces filled with people; an event silently taking place, and which will increase this formidable power more than half a dozen victories over the Turks.

From Rzeezyka I followed the course of the Nieper to Rohakzow, where I arrived the 12th; the distance more than fifty miles. The country is an open level plain, of fine meadow. I saw numerous villages deserted; and the fields, formerly arable, become pasture,

ture, but without cattle to graze them: all the inhabitants were moved into Ruffia. That town is the capital of a large province, the whole of which is in the hands of the Ruffians, who have three ftrong fortreffes in it, well garrifoned. Rohakzow is a fine town, beautifully fituated on the Nieper, on which its prefent mafters carry on a confiderable commerce. I much fufpect, from the fortifications raifed here by the Ruffians, whether the town or province will ever more be in the hands of the Poles. I was informed here, that much the greateft part of the province of Minfki, one of the moft confiderable in Lithuania, is entirely quiet, and in the abfolute power of the Ruffians; and where it will end, time can only know; but the prefent ftate of affairs in all this part of the world looks on every fide only in favour of the Ruffians; and it is certainly a moft ftrange infatuation, that the other powers of Europe fhould be mere ftanders-by, and look on to this great fuccefs of the Ruffians without thinking it their intereft to interfere. Auftria and Pruffia are armed, it is true; but the progrefs of this empire is of a kind which admits not open declarations from any but the Poles. I have heard it mentioned as a mark of very fagacious politicks in the Turks, that the real

reafon

reason of the present war with Ruffia is from a jealoufy of the Mufcovite power being too much increafed by the advantages taken of the troubles in Poland. The Porte thought there was danger of the Emprefs taking poffeffion of the whole kingdom of Poland in her own name; and judged that the beft way of preventing fuch a great acceffion to her power was by the fword cutting her out work elfewhere.

From Rohakzow, I reached Rychow the 13th; the diftance more than forty miles. All this country is very rich, and part of it very well cultivated, but it is in the hands of the Ruffians entirely; many of the peafants are of that nation, and every thing feen is a proof that this empire has much enlarged its bounds, without either a formal war, or even the authority of a treaty. This place is in the province of Miflau, a very fine and fertile country, an hundred miles long, and as many broad, and all in the hands of the Ruffians. The foil here is chiefly a reddifh loam; much of it is in culture, as was evident from the large tracks of ftubble I went through; but I faw no hemp, flax, or tobacco, thofe products being pretty much confined to the Ukraine. Rychow, with fome neighbouring towns, belong to a Polifh nobleman, driven away by the

the Ruffians, who have feized his whole eftate, and taken poffeffion of it in a manner that precludes the idea of his ever returning. From this place I rode about forty miles to Kudzin, through the fame province. All this line of country, I could fee, had been in general under culture, but it was now entirely wafte. I counted the remains of no lefs than feven villages, which were entirely deferted, all the inhabitants being fled to Ruffia. From Kudzin, the fame diftance brought me, on the 15th, to Krula, another little town, with a Ruffian garrifon. The country is partly cultivated, and partly deferted; but the remaining inhabitants will not be left here long; for I faw a Ruffian commandant, whofe bufinefs was, the taking an account of the people of feveral adjacent villages that had petitioned for lands in Ruffia. Thefe emigrations are not at all furprizing: in time of peace the Polifh nobles treat all the peafants as flaves in the utmoft extent of the word: when, therefore, a fcene of trouble and confufion comes, they are fure to take the firft opportunity to defert, that they may efcape in future the renewal of their former mifery; and the condition of the new fettlers in Ruffia is fo infinitely fuperior to that of the peafants in Poland, that nothing can exceed the eagernefs ness with which they all fly from the scene of their slavery the moment their masters are driven away. These are the effects of that tyranny which all the Polish nobility exert upon their vassals; so that in case the Russians should restore these numerous provinces, the Poles will return to deserts, instead of well-peopled estates.

The 16th I got to Obloka; the distance forty-six miles; still in the province of Mislaw. All this track is a fine rich country, but very poorly peopled, many villages being deserted. I passed a very large seat, belonging to a Polish nobleman, in ruins. Whoever declares against the Russian party, are sure to have their estates laid waste, and many of their peasants carried off; and in the provinces which lie near to the frontiers of that empire, they are driven away, and every thing seized by the enemy. There are not many finer countries than great part of this province, but it is in a desolate state. I have met with no parties of Poles, nor any appearance of war: the Empress has a quiet and effectual possession of much the greatest part of Lithuania; and such parts are the only ones in the kingdom that enjoy any repose.

The 17th I reached Whitepski, the capital town of a large province, also in the hands of the

the Ruffians. The country is very woody. In fifty miles, which were this day's journey, near thirty were through a continual foreft; the reft is tolerably well cultivated, and peopled; it is in poffeffion of fome Poles, who fecured themfelves from the beginning by declaring for the Ruffian caufe. They cultivate their own eftates by means of their vaffals, who have fmall cottages, with little plots of ground round them, in which they raife what is neceffary for the fubfiftence of themfelves and their families in three days of the week, which are allowed them, and the reft of the time they work for their lord, under the direction of overfeers. One of thefe noblemen cultivates in this manner above fix thoufand acres of land: his eftate contains above twenty thoufand acres, but much of it is marfh and foreft. This is a reprefentation of all the eftates in Poland in time of peace. The owners of them, however fmall, are all Polifh gentlemen, and entirely equal; but the numerous diftractions they have had from the beginning of their monarchy, have confolidated moft of the fmall properties, fo that at prefent the kingdom is generally divided into large eftates. Every owner cultivates his land by means of the peafants on it, who belong to him as much as the trees which

grow

grow on the foil; thus the Poles are the greateſt farmers in the world, for ſome of their princes poſſeſs whole provinces, containing ſeveral hundred thouſand acres of land, and all their revenue, which is very conſiderable, is raiſed by this cultivation. The principal value of eſtates is the vicinity to a navigable river; for without this advantage they have not a vent for the immenſe quantity of corn which they raiſe. The ſtubbles I ſaw upon the eſtate juſt now mentioned, were of all the common ſorts, and very extenſive, wheat, barley, oats, peaſe, beans, buck-wheat. I ſaw a few turneps, but the quantity did not ſeem to be any thing proportioned to the extent of corn.

In the night of the 17th the weather changed, which had hitherto favoured me ſo remarkably; very heavy rains fell with ſleet and ſnow, and continued ſo bad the next day, that I ſtaid at Whitepſki that day and the two following ones, in expectation of a froſt ſetting in, for they told me I ſhould find the roads much worſe and more liable to be damaged than thoſe I had paſſed. I ſtaid till the 20th, a very ſharp froſt having ſet in for four and twenty hours. The 21ſt I reached Goreſlaw, through fifty miles of foreſt; the 22d I got to Siteſky, the diſtance forty three miles; the ground hard frozen, and very good travelling,

velling, but the froft continues and the weather is fharp; this line of country, like the laft, is foreft. The 23d I reached Willifluki, which is in the boundary of Ruffia; but going from one country to the other makes no perceptible difference in the people, manners, or language; which is a circumftance that threatens the Poles not a little. I paffed through another colony of emigrants from that kingdom, who are feated on an eftate of the emprefs's, which came to her not long fince by forfeiture; it contains about four and twenty thoufand acres of land, and did not yield the late owner more than feven hundred pounds a year; but the Czarina will prefently make it twice as many thoufands, for there is the fineft timber for mafts on it that is to be found in all this country; and fhe is making a fmall ftream, that leads to the Iwanna, navigable; the expence will be but little; and fhe will carry her timber then to Petersburg by water, which will prove a moft important acquifition. The Polifh fettlement contains three hundred and forty farms, each a family; they had exactly the fame terms as thofe I gave an account of before.. They are feated in a plain thinly fcattered with trees, which they have cleared away: the foil I was informed, for I could

not

not fee it, is very deep and rich: they have each fifty acres divided by the Emprefs; and they have made many interior divifions. I was told that in Poland there are fcarcely any inclofures, but the Emprefs takes care that all the newly cultivated tracks in her dominions fhall be inclofed, being informed that they were the principal caufes which have fo much advanced the husbandry of England; and it is remarkable that the Poles fall very readily into it, and divide their fifty acres into feveral fields, as if they perfectly well underftood the importance of the conduct. They cultivate wheat, rye, oats, peafe, beans, and buckwheat; and have many crops of Swedifh turneps for the winter fupport of their cattle; they get two quarters of wheat and rye from an acre, but fometimes lefs; three of oats; and four of beans: and they reckon that an acre of turneps will winter two cows. It will be a prodigious advantage to this colony, the cutting a canal for the conveyance of the timber to Petersburg, for their products will find the fame way to a moft advantageous market. All thefe people are perfectly happy and contented; they are not deceived; on the contrary, they find their fituation to the full as good as they were made to expect; and they all speak of the Empress in the highest terms of admiration and gratitude.

This system of peopling her dominions is certainly the greatest exertion of politicks that she could possibly have shewn: other princes have been willing to increase the number of their subjects, by affording a refuge to emigrants in their dominions, but nothing else; whereas the Empress is at a considerable expence in planting them in hers; she spares no cost to make the number as great as possible; although from the cheapness of the country, it is done at, comparatively speaking, a small expence, yet when such numbers as she has thus received and settled are taken into the account, the sum of money annually expended in this truly noble way, will be found by no means small.

The 24th I reached Opolzko, the distance above forty miles; part of the country is forest, and part of it a level plain, or extended meadow, which did not seem to be marshy. I passed several villages, which seemed well peopled; and much of the country is tolerably cultivated. Opolzko is a fortified town, and stands in the middle of a small forest on a very pretty river; it is not large, but well built considering it is in Russia, where scarcely any thing is ever used but timber,

of

of which there is great plenty all over the empire. The 25th it snowed inceffantly, and so hard, that I was forced to stop till the 27th, before I could proceed on my journey; that is, till the snow which laid thick on the ground was frozen; and then I was provided with sledges, which are a very easy, expeditious, and agreeable way of travelling; and pleased me so exceedingly, that I wished for a longer journey on the snow than I now had to travel; the cold was not so penetrating as I expected to find it.

From Opolzko to Peterfburg, is two hundred and seventy miles, which I travelled in four days with great ease. And here ends this route through the western provinces of this great empire; which are the finest and most populous in it; for tho' I have been informed that Siberia, and other immense regions to the east, consist of as fertile a soil as any in the world, and some parts of them seated in as mild a climate, yet the near neighbourhood of the roving Tartars, in the southern and finest tracks, renders them almost continued deserts: Ruffia, it is true, has conquered many of them so completely, that they are not only tributary, but also entirely unable to exert themselves against the empire, nationally speaking; but with individuals the case is different, and those provinces could not be settled, without these Tartar neighbours being driven entirely away, or extirpated: so that the western provinces which are near to trade, and to the seat of government, are those of much the greatest importance: through these I have travelled above two thousand miles, so that I am able to form a pretty accurate general idea of the country.

It appears upon the whole, to be much better peopled than I expected to find it. It is true there are many forests in which you may travel a whole day without seeing any habitations; and in other parts of the empire, to a much greater extent; but we are not to look in Russia for the population of the most western countries of Europe; if such was to be found, this empire, which is of a much greater extent than that of the Romans, would be as powerful also; but the common ideas of this country being all a desart, are carried too far: It is very badly peopled, taking the whole together; but many of the provinces through which I passed are very populous: the towns are considerable, and the villages very thick; much of the territory in a good state of culture; and the appearance of it in many parts flourishing: to this may be added the great increase of people constantly gaining, by the

the reception and encouragement given to foreigners to fettle, who flock hither in whole troops: I fhall not affert that Ruffia is a populous well cultivated country; all I fay is, that there are more parts of it fo than I had reafon to expect from the accounts I had received, and the books I had read: the latter indeed muft neceffarily be far from the prefent truth in moft particulars, from the changes that are conftantly making, and from the improvements of all kinds which the prefent Emprefs fo nobly patronizes: and I may venture to predict, that if fhe enjoys a long life, fhe will change the face of the whole dominion; all the weftern provinces will be fully peopled: wherever the foil is fit for cultivation—the crown lands will be brought to yield a very great revenue, and general improvement fpread around.

Upon my arrival at Peterfburg I hired my old lodgings which had been empty fince I left them: I was not determined what courfe to take; bufinefs wanted me much in England, for I had received letters from three tenants in Northamptonfhire, complaining of my agent; and counter ones from my agent, complaining of my tenants; in which cafe, nothing is effectual but a landlord's prefence; on the contrary, the feafon was fo advanced, that it was impoffible to go by fea; and journeys in the

depth

depth of winter are to me extremely difagreeable, and the more fo, fince habit had made me attentive to the ftate of all the countries I paffed through, and inquifitive in examining the agriculture of them ; which is very badly performed in the midft of fnows : this made me think of fpending the winter at Peterfburg, and taking my way home in the fpring, either through Poland and Germany, or by the way of Turkey to the Adriatic, and fo to Italy; but not relifhing the idea of a winter, in latitude 60, I did not determine.

In this fufpence I fpent a fortnight, which time I paffed very agreeably, by means of a more extended acquaintance than I had made before ; and I was particularly happy in Mr. Mafon's arrival at Peterfburg, who had travelled quite acrofs Poland from Vienna ; he defigned to take advantage of the fnow, to travel through Siberia, a defign I much diffuaded him from : however, he determined on refting himfelf a month at Peterfburg ; and my being fo fortunate as to have much of this gentleman's company at my quarters, made the time and the feafon pafs away very agreeably: we converfed together upon the mutual fubject of our travels, which proved to me a fund of inexhauftible pleafure ; for Mr. Mafon, befides croffing Poland, had been all over Germany—

Germany—through part of Hungary; over Italy, France and Spain. He had been long upon this tour, and has contracted such a habit of moving about, that I believe he will not settle again, till he has travelled all the world over: Last winter he spent on the coast of Africa, and he has determined, for the sake of seeing the surprizing change, to pass this in the ice and snows of the north. This, it must be confessed, is seeing and becoming acquainted with human nature in every form, and with all the customs of the world; and to a person who has an inclination for such a way of life, which is strong in my friend Mr. Mason, it is pursuing the inclination effectually.

A person who lives genteely at Petersburg, especially if he be a foreigner, is sure to get easily into the best company in the court; I had not been six weeks settled in my winter habitation, before I had more company than I cared for; but it was not difficult to select from among them, some whose conversation was equally agreeable and instructive. And I never spent my time in a manner that was more to my inclination, than in the company of Mr. Mason, M. de Reversholt a general officer in the Russian service, a native of Saxony; the baron Minchewse a Russian nobleman,

nobleman, and the count de Selliern, a nobleman settled in Ruffia, but of Polifh extraction. Thefe men are perfectly well acquainted with the languages, courts, and armies of the principal nations in Europe. They have all travelled; are learned, polite, and of moft liberal ideas. For two months we took it by turns to have a dinner and fupper provided at our quarters, where all the reft affembled, and fpent the beft part of the day, and evening: the circle was fometimes enlarged by fome of us bringing a friend, which was chiefly three noblemen settled at Peterfburg, who introduced feveral Ruffian and other foreign officers, who had feen much fervice, and were polite and underftanding perfons. In this company I had the fatisfaction of having much converfation upon feveral fubjects of confequence, in which I was defirous of gaining further intelligence; particularly concerning the ftate of the diftant provinces of the empire, the views of the court upon the Black fea, and the prefent condition of the Turkifh forces.

M. de Reverfholt, who had been in the laft campaign againft the Ottomans, gave me the following particulars of the Turks, which I think may be agreeable to the reader:—He obferved, " that if ever the Ruffian empire

empire engaged in a war with a certainty of fuccefs, it is in the prefent; for the Turkifh army is perfectly enervated with peace; ten quiet years doing more mifchief to it in this refpect, than forty to any other army in Europe: the Janiffaries have the abfolute command of the empire; and their luxury and riot, in a time of peace, is fuch, being almoft without difcipline, that they reduce themfelves to a level with the worft forces in the Turkifh army. That, befides this evil, another of a yet worfe tendency is, the equality of the Grand Seignor's revenues: money in Turkey is of the fame cheapnefs as in all other countries of Europe, but the taxes of the empire continue always the fame; fo that the Turkifh monarch, although he has now the fame revenue as his predeceffors, ftill is beyond comparifon a much poorer prince. Many authors have given ftrange accounts that the Turkifh policy is fqueezing the bafhas, and by that means raifing a regular revenue; but he obferved, that it is a great miftake to think this any equivalent for the decline in the value of money; that now and then the Grand Seignor fleeces a bafha, and gets a confiderable fum, but in no refpect to be named with any regular revenue; that the forfeiture of eftates in Chriftian countries might almoft as well be

fet

set down for a revenue, as this of the Turks. He remarked, that the effects which were within the power of curious persons to become informed of, shewed that the revenue of the Turkish empire was smaller than in former times: one strong instance was the number of their troops being less, and this by so considerable a number as sixty thousand men. It is asserted as a fact, that the Grand Seignor cannot bring into the field so many men as the Ottoman armies consisted of forty years ago, by sixty thousand. Their artillery, while great improvements have been made through all the rest of Europe, has declined considerably; it does not consist of so many pieces as formerly, nor are the magazines of ammunition so well supplied. That in addition to this evil, the richest province of his empire, which is Egypt, is in a state of little less than rebellion; and the war with Russia bears so heavy on them, that they dare not call for a categorical declaration, almost knowing that it would denounce nothing but war.

In opposition to this picture, he enlarged upon the state of Russia, which, instead of being a declining, is really a rising power; that the Empress's army never was in so good order, nor so numerous as at present; that the

the troops were veterans, and not such as had, in a hot and luxurious climate, flept away their time in peace, but fresh from a vigorous service—men who scarcely knew what peace was. The success, continued he, which we have already had, shews that there is a great difference in the principle of this war from any former one between the two empires. It was the business of two or three campaigns to prepare for the war, and gain a situation from which the enemy might be attacked. Our armies fought to infinite disadvantage; they had an immense march across desarts to make, in order to get at the enemy; and, after a campaign, as long a march back to get at winter quarters: but now the scene has been changed; the northern shore of the Euxine is gained; conquests made in Moldavia and other Turkish provinces; so that the war is pushed at once into the enemy's country, and winter quarters gained there, which is precisely the thing that was always wanting before; and therefore the possession of it at present can hardly fail of being attended with the most fortunate consequences. I think it would be no extravagance to predict the fall of the Turkish empire being not very far off."

The

The Count de Minchewſe was of a different opinion from M. de Reverſholt in ſeveral converſations on this ſubject; and the arguments he uſed were to the following purport: —" I cannot contradict, ſaid that nobleman, the fact of our arms having a better proſpect of ſucceſs in this war than in any former one; but there are two circumſtances which appear to me ſufficiently ſtrong to prevent any ſuch brilliant ſucceſs as my friend mentions. Firſt, by beating the Turks, and carrying on two or three campaigns, their army will be daily improved, while no ſucceſs can make ours better than when they began the war. In every war which the Ottoman empire or the Houſe of Auſtria have carried on againſt us, they have improved in the ſucceſs of their arms from the continuance of the war; their raw, undiſciplined troops become veterans, and order and courage introduced among them from experience. This circumſtance makes a long and protracted war dangerous in itſelf, or at leaſt more favourable to the enemy than it can be to us. The revenues alſo of the two empires, though there is much truth in what has been aſſerted, ſtill will not bear a compariſon relative to the conduct of a war. The Grand Seignor can certainly ſupport great expences longer than the

the Emprefs; and, what is of much greater confequence, his fituation will ever make one ruble go as far as our five; for the Black fea keeps open a conftant navigation for fupporting their armies directly from their grand magazine, Conftantinople; and which will always be of great fervice, though a Ruffian fleet was upon that fea; but if they were deprived of that advantage, yet there is no comparifon between the eafe of recruiting the Turkifh armies with the beft troops from their provinces immediately at their backs, and the immenfe diftance which every thing from Ruffia has to go before it can arrive at our army; and this, I think, is almoft fufficient to prevent any very important fuccefs. All thefe points can hardly fail of making a protracted war more fatal to us, by the greatnefs of the expence, than it can be to the Turks. As to making a very bold pufh to finifh the war in two or three campaigns, by aiming fpeedily at Conftantinople, there are too many dangers in the plan to think that any commander would hazard it. From the two great frontier fortreffes, Ockzakow and Bender, there are near four hundred miles to Conftantinople. The Danube, with its fix mouths, and vaft marfhes, befides a great line of fortreffes, all lie in the way; and after that,

near

near three hundred miles of a very defensible country. Such a march must, in the nature of the proposition, leave all the provinces to the west of Moldavia and Wallachia behind; so that nothing would be easier than a Turkish army to be collected in those provinces, and to cut off the communication and retreat of the grand army: in such a situation it would be almost impossible for it to escape ruin. The Turks would have nothing to do but to destroy the country, harrass its march, and dispute every inch of land, and every post, still avoiding a general engagement: the least error in the Russian general would be destruction, and nothing but continued and signal victories could be crowned with success. In such a situation, I am not clear that the taking Constantinople would be decisive. But the war could never be carried on upon this plan; none is feasible but making absolutely sure of all the country as you advance; to leave nothing behind you unconquered, or unpossessed; but to advance slowly, campaign after campaign. If ever we are able to make any impression of consequence upon the empire of the Ottomans, it must certainly be in this method."

This discourse I thought carried with it great marks of knowledge, and a very attentive eye to the chances of the prefent war with the Turks; and I muft again repeat, what I obferved upon another occafion, that whenever a perfon, who minutes the obfervations he has made in his travels, has the fatisfaction of meeting with perfons thus capable of yielding inftruction, it may be as ufeful to take notes of their opinions as of his own; and accordingly I have feldom failed doing it. Upon revifion, I am inclined to own, that fuch parts of my memorandums have greater value than I fhould have been able to have given them.——I afked the baron, if he did not think that events of great importance might attend a victorious Ruffian fleet in the Euxine? He replied, I do not fee that events, fuch as we have been fpeaking of, can ever arife from it, except in one cafe; and the poffibility or probability of that muft depend on circumftances, of which we are all ignorant till they are tried. In making a conqueft of the Crim, or of the provinces to the north of the Danube, and to awe and curb the Tartars in the Turkifh alliance; in all thefe cafes, a victorious fleet would be of infinite importance, and give advantages to our arms which no other circumftances could. But I do not apprehend it poffible for any fleet to force its way through the Streights, and attack Conftantinople ſtantinople by water. But if the fleet on the Black ſea was numerous enough to take on board the whole Ruſſian army, with all its camp, baggage, artillery, proviſions, &c. I know not whether it would not be poſſible to land them within two or three days march of Conſtantinople; nay, in caſe the coaſt is favourable to diſembarking, in one day's march. In this caſe, the expedition would not be in the abſolute danger of miſcarrying from a march of four hundred miles, with a certainty of the retreat being cut off, but the event thrown at once on that of a battle, in a ſituation where a victory, ſupported and maintained by ſuch a fleet, would probably overthrow the empire; for there is a wide difference between gaining ſuch a victory freſh from the ſhips, and ſo ſupported, and the ſame ſucceſs without any ſupport, and after the repeated and certain loſſes of a long and deſperate march. But to ſuch a ſcheme there would be many objections, though not ſo ſtrong as to the other: the greateſt would be the difficulty of procuring, manning, and ſupporting ſuch a fleet as would be neceſſary to make the conduct at all ſecure; and this is ſo great, that it would never be poſſible to effect, in conſequence of events that fell out after a war began; for many years would be neceſ-

ſary

sary for the mere building such a fleet, and great treasures must be expended in it. It could never therefore be executed without the idea being conceived in a time of peace, and the fleet built in consequence, and ready for use, with skilful mariners and pilots ready at the breaking out of the war: which state of the case supposes the Empress to be in possession of all the north coast of that sea, and to have the free navigation of it; for without both, it would be impossible to think of the execution of such a plan. Thus you see what long preparation must in any case be necessary to form a consistent plan for attacking Constantinople; and yet I am persuaded that this is the only plan that can ever prove successful. First, there must be a war, and a successful one; for such must be that which gives possession of Little Tartary and the Crim to the Empress. After this war, no time should be lost in raising a naval force upon the Black sea, superior to any thing the Turks can fit out. Thirdly, that sea must be most minutely navigated, that every ship may have a pilot who knows the rocks, banks, currents, &c. And lastly, a succeeding war must happen so successful, as to put us in possession of the provinces north of the Danube; for even by sea it might be fatal

fatal to make the attempt with a strong enemy left behind so near as Ockzakow, Bender, or any places in that country.—When all these previous steps were taken, and had proved succefsful, then I should suppose the attempt might be made, and with a probability of succefs. I do not speak of the practicability of landing on the south-west coast of the Euxine, because I have been often told that it is all a very safe coast, and proper for landing on."

The whole month of December, and the beginning of January 1770, we spent in our mutual visits at Petersburg; and I may say with great truth, and without paying the other members a compliment, that I never passed any time more agreeably: now and then Mr. Mason and myself appeared at court, which is necefsary here; and the Emprefs learning that we were great travellers, entered more than once into conversation with us; and enquired into our opinions of several objects we had viewed. She is reserved in the manner of her speech, but has a noble open countenance, with a becoming greatnefs in her air and carriage. There is nothing lively or pleasing at court, the whole being but a dull tho' a fine scene. It is certain that the great wisdom which has hitherto appeared

in

in all the actions and councils of this princefs, flows from her own perfonal genius and abilities: I have not learned that fhe has any minifters, whofe diftinguifhed parts would give one any reafon to fuppofe the fuccefs owing to them; befides, it is well known here, that the Emprefs is very determinate in her opinion. She afks and hears the advice of her council upon important affairs; but fhe generally follows her own opinion, which is evident from her acting directly contrary to the opinion of the whole in two or three affairs of confequence; and in which the fuccefs that followed, proved clearly that her own judgment was better than that of all her minifters. She is remarkable for being exceeding quick in her decifions; fhe never acts from long and repeated confideration, but determines almoft inftantaneoufly, and executes with equal celerity. Such a difpofition is certainly fitter for the conduct of great affairs, than one in which more caution, and a greater degree of prudence appeared; for nothing is fo fatal in the government of an empire, as inconftancy and irrefolution. He who confiders long before he determines, muft infallibly mifs many opportunities, which to more active minds are feized the inftant they appear.

The last week in January, Mr. Mason informed me that he had determined on an excursion into Siberia on the snow, and attempted to persuade me to accompany him; I did not like the scheme, as it must prove a long and tedious journey; and in my turn, I proposed an excursion wherever he pleased for a month, which would give us both an opportunity of seeing the nature of this travelling; we conversed often upon this subject before we could decide; as we presently determined to break the length of the winter, by some excursion of this sort. I expatiated to him upon the dreariness of so long a journey upon the snow, and offered to accompany him to Ispahan, in Persia; which was moving into a warm climate, instead of freezing on the snows of the north; besides, such a plan would shew us a country highly worthy of our attention, and introduce us into quite a new scene. He objected to taking such a journey in the depth of winter, asserting, and truly, that to have it agreeable, it should be made in the spring. At last he came into the scheme of a short excursion; and that we might have the snow in perfection, he determined to point full north, and visit Archangel, and the coast of the White sea.

As this journey was more a scheme of amusement than observation; and as it was performed while the ground was covered several feet deep with frozen snow, it afforded very little matter that is worthy of registering in this journal. We crossed the lake of Ladoga, upon the ice and snow to Oloucky, thence cross the lake Onega to Cargapol, and from thence through a great forest to Archangel. The distance is about three hundred miles, which took us only five days; we stopped for lodgings at the towns we passed; and the scenery of the country, which exhibited a world of snow in every phantastic form that can be imagined, was a source of perpetual amusement. The weather was very severe; but it is incredible how warm a compleat suit of fur, well surrounded with cloaks of the same, keeps one; I believe I could have slept all night upon the snow, and full in the keenest wind, without any other covering than my furs; but travelling in cold countries has made me hardy; Mr. Mason often complained, when I felt not the least inconvenience. The smooth and immense plain formed on the two lakes, is an object amazingly striking; and the vast forests rising out of the snow in some places, and in others covered with it, exhibited scenes infinitely magnificent

nificent. I had many opportunities of seeing the winter life of the peasants, the inhabitants of lonely cottages in the midst of these unbounded snowy regions. They lay in a store for winter of salted meat indiscriminately of whatever sort they have; also a quantity of rye, barley, pease or meal; and they lay up likewise, a considerable portion of dried fish, which they cure in the smoak of their cabbins: this winter stock, with the fowls and accidental beasts they kill in ranging the forests, supply them tolerably well. They cloath themselves very warm in the skins of ordinary sorts of beasts, that hardly deserves the name of furs: and the plenty of wood every where to be found, makes firing so cheap an article to them, that their winter lives I take to be much more comfortable than their summer ones; for their lords have not so much work for them to perform, so that more of their time is their own; the greatest regale that can be given them is that of a dram; and we have often found, that they would in any little contract perform much more than they agree to, if a dram is added. This in so cold a country, and where the articles of luxury among the poor are so extremely limited, is not to be wonder'd at.

Archangel

Archangel is a small town, almost on the mouth of the Divini, which river is very broad, and deep, and forms an excellent harbour. It contains about five thousand inhabitants, but the number once was near thirty thousand, when it was the great staple of all the trade which the English and Dutch carried on with Russia, before Peter the great founded Petersburg. It is worthy of observation, that from that port there was a considerable export of Russian commodities, particularly naval stores and furs, before that great commerce was in being, which has since arose at Petersburg. In those days it was not an uncommon thing to see three or four hundred sail of ships at a time in this harbour, but now very few resort there: It is a poor place; the buildings containing nothing that is at all worthy of notice: They have a cathedral, and an archbishop of the Greek church; but every thing looks much on the decline.

To avoid returning to Petersburg by the same road we had come, Mr. Mason proposed our crossing the White sea on the ice, and taking a small compass through Lapland, and turning southwards round that sea down to the lake Ladoga, and so home to Petersburg: this plan I readily agreed to, and accordingly we executed it. From the promontory of
Catsnoze,

Catfnoze, acrofs to Parfiga in Lapland, is about feven and thirty miles, which we paffed in lefs than a day, though not without fome danger. From thence we went to Pohina, then to Kola, almoft on the north fea, and turning fouth to Keretta, paffed out of Lapland from Kovoda, into Carelia, having travelled near five hundred miles through Mufcovite Lapland. I expected to find nine tenths of the country a defart; but it is not fo; on the contrary there are feveral little towns, and among thofe on the coaft there is a fmall trade divided; a fhip on a coafting voyage now and then comes in fummer, to purchafe furs with fuch commodities as are moft in requeft among the Laplanders. There is very little cultivation among them; but they have large orchards, which furnifh them with an ordinary fort of apple: what corn they fow, is chiefly rye, and a little barley; and this is a new thing, for formerly they lived entirely upon hunting and fifhing, which are at prefent their principal dependance; they dry both flefh and fifh for winter provifion, and feem not much to regard the feverities of the climate. I do not enter into any particular defcription of them, or their manners, becaufe I find that the accounts which I have read are very juft. The face of the country,

from

from what could be seen of it in this season, cannot be disagreeable; it consists of many open plains, gentle hills, and woods; some of which are open groves, having no underwood in them. This province pays the Empress but one tax, which is a certain tribute of furs; the amount of which is considerable. The rental of the estates, which are situated in it, is paid entirely in furs and skins, for which the peasants have liberty to cultivate whatever land they want, and also to hunt and fish on all the estates. In such a country it may be supposed, that large tracks of land yield but very small returns; I was assured afterwards by a gentleman at Petersburg, that he has a track of sixty miles long, by four and twenty broad in some places, and the income of it was not four hundred pounds a year neat at Petersburg.

Upon our return to that city, we renewed our former society in order to pass the rest of the winter in as agreeable a manner as possible; a purpose, which I found was fortunately answered, and made me often reflect with pleasure on my determining to winter here. But I believe, much in such cases is to be attributed to one's determining beforehand to make the best of all those inconveniencies which may be occasioned by difference of climate or season.

season. In the depth of winter the inhabitants of Russia keep chiefly within doors; the society of the fire-side is then the only refuge from the inclemency of the weather: this naturally begets a more sociable temper; and a greater willingness to be pleased, than if all common objects divided the attention and occupied one's hopes and fears. Whether this is or is not a rational account of the matter, I have however often experienced the case; and tho' my acquaintance this winter at Petersburg wanted no circumstances to set them off, yet I think I enjoyed their conversation more, than if it had been in the midst of the mildness of a winter in Andalusia.

The count de Sellirne informed us the middle of March, that he should very early in the spring repair by the Empress's order to Azoph, to make the campaign which was meditated against the Turks in Georgia; and in which he expected a commission of importance. This turned our conversation for several days on the views of the court of Russia, in the war in that part of the world; and the Baron Minchewse asserted, that attacking the Turks in their provinces, between the Black sea and the Euxine, was one of the wisest measures that could be adopted, and the best calculated of any to give a great diversion to

their

their arms, to the eafe of the war in the provinces on the north of the Danube. It is a territory of very great importance, from its fituation between the two feas, as well as from the finenefs of the climate and the fertility of much of the foil. It is by means of thefe provinces that they hold fo great a command of the Black fea, entirely furrounding it by their dominions and ports. By thefe provinces alfo, the communication is kept up between their other dominions, and the Tartars in fubjection or alliance with them, after the Ruffian army cuts it off on the weftern coaft. Such a diverfion, if made by an army tolerably powerful, would have great effects; thofe eaftern provinces are weak, drained of their troops, and the fortreffes never in good order; if all the maritime ones were attacked one after another by an army in concert with a fleet, the war might in two campaigns be carried to the fouthern coaft of that fea, which would alarm the Turks exceedingly, and occafion great drafts from their grand army.

Upon another occafion, when we were converfing upon the profpects of the prefent war, I related the journey I had made from the Ukraine along the frontiers of Poland to Peterfburg; and obferved, that an immenfe track

track of country was not only in the hands of the Ruffian troops, but the towns and villages partly peopled with Ruffians, while the old inhabitants were all flying into Ruffia: this, I remarked, had all the appearance of the Emprefs's defigning to annex thofe countries to her dominions. The Count faid, in reply, that there were feveral provinces in Lithuania which the ancient Czars had long claimed; they were once independent; and after putting themfelves firft under the protection of Poland, then under that of Ruffia, and then going back to Poland again, difputes about the fovereignty had happened, which extended in fome degree to the whole grand duchy of Lithuania: he therefore fuppofed the Emprefs might keep thofe provinces in her hands, if not retain them, at leaft for making a divifion with the republick, and afcertaining clearly the boundary, if ever a time of tranquillity fhould return. He faid that there was great reafon to believe fo very political a princefs would not miftake fo much, as to form any confiderable conquefts from Poland, and that for two unanfwerable reafons: firft, becaufe they are not to her worth having, after the inhabitants are all fwept away; by her encouragements fhe attracts the greater part, and fear fends away the reft: if, on a

peace,

peace, the owners of thofe provinces are at the trouble to re-people them from other parts of Poland, they will only be at work for her, as in a future rupture the fame game will be played over again, and the Emprefs gain every thing fhe wants, which is not territory, but people. The fecond reafon is no lefs forcible; if fhe was to difmember any provinces of confequence from the kingdom of Poland, fhe would fcarcely fail of bringing the united arms of Auftria and Pruffia on her; neither of which powers can ever fee, with any degree of fatisfaction, the increafe of this empire's greatnefs, and would declare againft it the inftant any appearance took place of making acquifitions from Poland, which to them would carry appearances of greater defigns; and if Poland fell into the hands of any neighbour, the ballance of power in all this part of the world is at once deftroyed; and of all events, none can be more againft the interefts of Auftria and Pruffia, than to bring the Ruffian power nearer to them than it is at prefent. Peopling her waftes is the great object of the Czarina; Polifh provinces would be of no value to her; if territory is her object, it cannot be in Poland, but on the Euxine fea, where it would bring trade, and a command with it, of much more confequence to her than half of Poland. The Ruffians you faw fettling on the frontier provinces, muft be merely fuch as are attracted by the armies with a view of fupplying them, at a time when the deferted houfes and farms of the Poles were ready to receive them; but they will all be glad to return when the occafion of their going is removed. Thofe provinces are now under the civil as well as military adminiftration of Ruffia, which muft of confequence carry a great number of Ruffians there, whofe refidence can be no longer than the occafion continues. All will return upon a general pacification.

I fhould think, in good politics, the Count's opinion muft be right; and that the Emprefs keeps poffeffion of fo many Polifh provinces, in order to be better able to carry off all the inhabitants; which is certainly making the beft ufe of them that can be to her. But, at the fame time, fhe acquires all that ftrength which would be the confequence of feizing the provinces themfelves; and therefore her rivals, who would declare againft her for one, fhould, to be confiftent, do the fame for the other; for there certainly can be no doubt but the increafe of a million of fubjects, fixed on the crown lands of this empire, would ftrengthen the monarch on the throne far

more

more than the acquisition of a Polish province, containing a million, and yield four or five times the wealth.

The approach of the spring made Mr. Mason and myself think of leaving Petersburg. He determined to travel into Persia, and, if the country is tolerably settled, to go by land through the Mogul's empire to our settlements on the coast of Coromandel; an idea very worthy of a man who, I believe, will never cease to travel till he ceases to live. But as I have no desire to pass away my life without the satisfaction of fixing, I shall bend my course homewards, with the pleasing idea of turning a country farmer in Northamptonshire, and putting in practice, on my own estate, some of the various cultures and methods which I have viewed in so many places.

The 3d of April, 1770, I left Petersburg, taking with me five attendants to conduct me safe through Poland; among whom were two soldiers, who could speak German and Polish: of the former language I have enough to understand common conversation. Such a retinue in England would cost a traveller four or five pounds a day; but I could travel in Russia or Poland for four and thirty shillings a day, all expences included, except extraordinary ones: when I ftop at large towns, the landlords, though they are very reafonable, will yet fwell the account higher than that. I arrived the 5th at Narva, which is one hundred miles; the country very badly inhabited, but much of it cultivated. The froft is beginning to go; fo in ten days or a fortnight we may expect fummer, which, in the northern climates, comes at once, without the intervention of fpring. The fnow melts apace; till it is quite gone, the roads will be bad; but I have even, in their prefent circumftances, travelled on worfe.

Narva is prettily fituated on the banks of a fine river, though not a deep one, as fhips of any fize cannot come up to the town: it is well built, and ftrongly fortified. Here is a confiderable trade in hemp, flax, timber, potafhes, and moft of the commodities which are exported from Peterfburg. Almoft all the trade is in the hands of the Englifh and Dutch; but the former are much the greateft purchafers: the trade which the latter carry on here has long been on the decline. I left Narva the 6th, at noon, and taking the banks of the river, followed it two days, when I arrived at Salatíki, which is above ninety miles from Narva, ftanding at the bottom of a very fine lake, above forty miles broad, and as much long.

long. All this country is pretty well cultivated. I faw many fields of rye beautifully green, though fo lately covered with fnow, and much of them now under it. The 8th I reached Plefcow, on a lake of the fame name, fome parts of which, from the wooded iflands which are thick in it, are very beautiful. All this country is as well cultivated as any part of Ruffia. It produces a large quantity of flax; but they reckon the foil rather too light for hemp. They have two feafons for fowing both wheat and rye; October, and April and May; but they reckon that the former feafon yields the beft produce. They grow much more corn than is neceffary for their own confumption, which, with their flax, is exported by the port of Narva; water carriage giving them that opportunity at a very cheap rate. Wheat yields here two quarters, and fometimes more, upon an acre; rye not more than wheat: barley is not fown till the middle of May, but the heat of the fun brings an early harveft; it is not reckoned a very profitable grain here; they get from two quarters to two and an half per acre: oats yield three and an half. I had been informed, that in Livonia, one method of cultivation was very extraordinary, which was, that of flooding vales that would admit it, and keeping them

them as fish-ponds for three or four years, and then, letting the water off, they cultivate it for corn for five or six years; after which the water must be let on again to fertilize it afresh: but on enquiry I found it was not in this part of the country: but they use here almost as many wood ashes for manuring their lands as they do in Sweden, and say that no other manure has so great an effect.

The roads growing but indifferent, I did not reach Marienburg till the 10th; the distance better than fifty miles. The country is woody in parts, but much of it very well cultivated. I passed through large tracks of young wheat and rye, which looked extremely well; and the peasants were all busy in the fields with their ploughs, which they work, some with horses, and some with oxen. They were tilling their lands for barley and oats, and also flax; for the latter of which they appropriate their best soils, if not wet clays; but they prefer a fine light sandy loam for it. An acre of good flax is worth from three to five pounds; but they raise much that does not yield three. Marienburg is a small town, tolerably well built, and most romantically situated on a promontory of land which projects into a large lake; so that it is joined to the main land only by a narrow neck, not

much

much wider than the road. An inland place in a country not full of manufactures, can scarcely be of any great importance. Marienburg was once of consequence for its strength, and the scene of several military expeditions, when belonging to the Teutonic knights. It is at present poor, but strong for this part of the world. The people live cheaply, from the fertility of the neighbouring country, and the vast quantity of fish which they get out of the lake. The farmers manure their land around the lake with a kind of ouze, which they dig up on the banks of it: it is of a deep blue colour, about two feet deep, cuts like wet peat, and is composed of rotten vegetables; for there is an immense growth of weeds every year in the lake, which drive ashore and rot, and, with a mixture of mud, forms this manure, which is of the nature of marle, and fertilizes their fields for many years. I have no doubt but the same materials might be found on the coasts of many other lakes; but custom not having made the use of them common, the husbandmen neglect them.

The 11th I got to Pebalgen, another town built on a lake; the distance about forty miles, through a territory, part good, and part of it marshy; but all the lands that would admit of culture, seemed to be under cultivation, and yielded wheat, rye, barley, oats, and pulse. They also cultivate cabbages for the winter food of their herds, which are very numerous. It is a large red cabbage, which stands the utmost severity of the winter, and is taken from under the snow in full perfection for all sorts of cattle, who are wonderfully fond of them. They used to sow the Swedish turnep for this use, but come more into the cabbage, from finding the produce much greater. As to its standing the winter, from the observations I have made, I am inclined to believe the climates in which vegetables suffer most, are not those where great quantities of snow fall, but such as have severe frosts without any snow: the snow keeps them warm, and greatly protects them from the keen frosty winds, which in other countries cut off so many vegetables. There is not much flax in this line of country; but they cultivate a little hemp: however they depend most upon common husbandry. It is remarkable that there is a great difference between Livonia, and the other parts of Russia which I have been in. The ancient provinces generally are divided into the estates of the nobility, who cultivate them by means of stewards and agents, the peasants being all slaves. But

in

in the Ukraine, the land belongs to little freeholders, if I may so call them, who cultivate their own property. Now in Livonia the case differs from both; for here estates are of all sizes, and let out upon farming leases, as in England. There are many seats of country gentlemen, who all have a part of their estates in their own hands; but the peasants, though not so much at their ease as in free countries, yet are not enslaved; they hire large tracks of land, which some of them cultivate extremely well; and many of them are worth considerable sums of money for this part of the world.

The 12th I rode near fifty miles to Cropper, through a country most beautifully watered with small lakes and rivers; it is diversified with gentle hills and groves of fine trees, and great part of it well cultivated; many parts of England have a much worse appearance. The peasants from the general activity seen among them, I take to be a very industrious set of people; scarcely any arable field but what had ploughs at work in it; the soil is sandy, for loams and clays require some time to dry after the snow is gone, before they will admit the cattle to till it; but these lands inclinable to sand are presently dry enough for tillage; they plough variously for their spring corn, some only once, others three times. Flax is cultivated by many of them; but they assured me that wheat paid them better, though some farmers have now and then such good flax-crops as induces them to continue the culture. I remarked that most of them are very attentive through the winter season in raising dunghills, or rather compost heaps near their houses; for there was scarcely a farm without a great square heap piled up to a considerable height; they are composed of the dung of their cattle, which they winter in houses, and litter them with rushes and other aquatic weeds, which they cut up for that purpose in their numerous lakes and rivers; they also add great quantities of mud, also wood ashes, &c. and at this time of the year, they mix these hills together, turning them over, and incorporating the ingredients; after which they leave them, till they sow barley or plant cabbages, spreading them on the land before the last ploughing. This must all be a very excellent system of husbandry.

The 13th in the afternoon I reached Riga which is the most considerable place for trade next to Petersburg in the Russian dominions. It stands very advantageously for commerce, near the mouth of the river Dwina, which, with its branches extending a great way into Poland

Poland and Ruſſia, bring immenſe quantities of commodities which are exported from this city: Among theſe the principal are hemp, flax, timber for maſts and other purpoſes; pitch, tar, and pot aſhes; all theſe commodities are produced in the provinces or near them, through which thoſe rivers run; and ſome of them by means of ſhort land carriage from one river to another, much further even from the Ukraine and the Poliſh provinces that border upon Turkey. It appears by the regiſters of the cuſtom-houſe at this town, that more than five hundred ſail of ſhips, from one hundred and fifty to four hundred tons, have been loaded here in a year; three hundred of which were Dutch, and one hundred and ſixty Engliſh; but of late the trade of the town has declined, for at preſent there are not many more than four hundred ſail cleared outwards, of which about two hundred and forty are Engliſh. Every ton of the goods they carry from hence, might be had at our own plantations; but for want of due encouragement we come to Ruſſia for them, and pay ſome hundred thouſand pounds bailance on the account; which is an inſtance of miſtaken politicks that never was to be equalled in the annals of the Dutch republick.

I had

I had a letter of recommendation to Mr. Scueen, a principal merchant in this town, with whom I spent the evening; and he not only gave me the heads of the preceding particulars, but I had also some instructive converfation with him on the prefent ftate of the province of Livonia. Of all Peter the great's conquefts, this was the moft important; being a country which for its products, ports and fituation is of the higheft importance to Ruffia. It forms upon an average, a fquare of 200 miles every way, and contains better than twenty five millions of acres, and near a million of people. Above half the lands he calculates, are under profitable cultivation, either in arable crops or good meadow; and exclufive of woods, marfhes, lakes and rivers. The annual product is about thirteen millions fterling, including timber. Such an eftimate cannot be accurate, I do not give it the reader as a paper of authority; it is nothing more than the calculation of a very ingenious fenfible man, who has many times travelled all over Livonia. The parts which I faw are not equal in culture to others in the province, yet I fhould apprehend that half the track I came through is under culture, meadows included; and as to the number of acres, it is a geographical fact. But I fhould not conceive

ceive there were quite a million of people in it; I heard the number once eftimated at between fix and feven hundred thoufand. Suppofing ten or twelve millions of acres cultivated, which does not appear to me an exaggerated idea; I do not fee how the total product of the province can be eftimated fo low as thirteen millions. But from this fketch of particulars, it is eafy to conceive that the importance of the province to Ruffia is very great.

Travels

Travels thro' Poland and Pruſſia.

Journey to Dantzick—Description of the country and husbandry—Trade of Dantzick—Journey to Warsaw—Miserable state of Poland—To Breslaw.

THE 14th I left Livonia, and reached Mittaw, the capital of Courland, the distance about eight and forty miles. The face of the country is exactly the same as that of Livonia, and the soil equally fruitful, which by information I found was the case of the whole dutchy: their products, as hemp, flax, lintseed, timber, masts, pot-ash, skins, tar, honey, wax, &c. are considerable. The whole country is full of black cattle, and they have many horses. Mittaw was in the happy times of the dukes of Courland, when the Ketler family had quiet possession, and before the dutchy and all its towns were ravaged by the Swedes and Muscovites, it was then a considerable and a fine town; it reckoned fifteen thousand inhabitants, but now they are not more than nine thousand. It is yet an agreeable place, well built with a handsome ducal palace, where is something of a court with guards,

guards, and there is always a strong garrison in it. Of late years there have been great additions to the fortifications. It is now, as well as the whole dutchy, in the hands of the Russians.

From Mittaw, I reached Zagari in Poland on the 15th, being about four and forty miles; part of the country tolerably cultivated, but not equal to Livonia, or even to Courland; there were some Russian soldiers at Zagari to keep the town and the neighbouring country in order, which they do very effectually; and a great advantage it is to these parts of Poland, where the civil war is thus kept under by a foreign power. The advantages of all the cultivation I saw are in the hands of the Russians, for the Polish nobles through most of the great province of Samogitia are driven from their estates, and the profits of such of them as are not depopulated all go to the Russians. The cottages of the peasants are as mean as can well be conceived; they are chiefly built of turf, and covered with the same, being drawn up in a spiral form to a point, where is an aperture for the smoak to go out; the room is large enough for the family and the cattle; all lye together and in the same manner. I had read that they used in this province none

but

but wooden plough-fhares, through a ridiculous notion that the iron damaged their crops; but this is not true, for I faw many ploughs at work for barley, and all of them had iron fhares, but of a moft aukward conftruction.

The 16th I got to Rofenne, the diftance near fixty miles; through a country that had hardly any appearance of prefent cultivation; many villages I paffed that were deferted, feveral manfions in ruins, and fields entirely wafte that had once been tilled; the whole a very melancholy fpectacle; but much of the country was partly marfh and foreft. The town of Rofenne is a fmall fortified place, which has a Ruffian garrifon; there is an appearance of nothing but poverty in it. The 17th I got to Swingy, a little town about thirty four miles from Rofenne; there is fome land in this line of country under cultivation, being the eftate of a nobleman who enjoys it in tolerable peace under the protection of Ruffia. They fow barley, oats, peafe, beans, and a little rye; I faw feveral ploughs at work; and upon examining them, found that the fhares were wood, to my no fmall furprize; I enquired the reafon of this, and they could give me none, only that they never ufed any other fort; the land here is fandy, and did not

feem

seem to yield good crops: the rye was full of weeds; I asked if it was to be weeded, and they told me they never weeded any corn at all. The nobleman is an old man, who has his estate managed in the same way as his father had; that is, the peasants are miserably oppressed by his stewards, and his own income at the same time contemptible.

The 18th I travelled forty miles to Stocken, all in Prussia, the country sandy, and not much of it well cultivated, but the peasants are much more at their ease than in Poland, and this country being subject to the king of Prussia, no Russians, no Polish confederacies nor any disturbances happen in it, which is a very great advantage to agriculture; tho' I yet have seen nothing that gives me any great idea of their knowledge in that science. This country is much more populous than Samogitia, and the houses of the peasants built of much better materials. I passed two or three villages entirely inhabited by Poles who have fled their country, and settled here by order of the king of Prussia; though without any of that noble encouragement I saw exerted in Russia; and I believe those who take refuge in the latter country, are in other respects better treated than they are in Prussia. The 19th I got by dinner to Koningsburg, the distance

stance being only twenty miles through a country pretty well cultivated, and tolerably peopled, though the foil is in general fandy, and from its appearance I should not apprehend it very good. All the country people were now bufy in preparing their land for fpring fown corn; they plough here with only two cattle in a plough; and I faw fome drawn by a little horfe and a cow; or a little ox; this is very practicable with fo light a foil: they fow large quantities of buckwheat, and reckon it more profitable than barley. Koningfburg is the moft confiderable town which the King has in Pruffia; it is tolerably well fituated, and has a very good harbour with fome trade, but not near equal to that of Riga, though it is a hanfe town. The export is in the fame articles, except hemp and flax, of which the quantity is too inconfiderable to mention. Upon the coaft are found fometimes large quantities of yellow amber, which is to be bought at Koningfburg. The ftreets are broad, but irregular and not well paved; but there are many very good buildings in it, and they reckon above twenty thoufand inhabitants. The King has made feveral attempts to increafe its trade, but they do not feem to be attended with any great effect. Dantzick, on one fide, and Riga on the other, are two fuch rivals,

rivals, that this place cannot make its trade good againſt them for any thing further than the mere amount of the products of that track of country, which lies nearer to it than to any other.

The 20th I reached Ladſperg, at about forty miles from Koningſburg: the country all ſandy, and, that circumſtance conſidered, pretty well inhabited. Buck-wheat is a great crop with them, I found. They do not ſow it till the end of May: the produce is greater than that of any other grain or pulſe, and the ſtraw they reckon nearly equal to hay for cattle; an obſervation I had not any where heard of before. The peaſants of this country, I find, are all much freer than in Poland, but they pay very heavy taxes to the King; yet they are not in ſuch bad circumſtances as the Poliſh peaſants, becauſe taxation is regular; whereas the payments made by the peaſants to their lords in Poland, are ſo capricious, that they never know when they have paid their total: moſt of it being in cattle, and irregular perſonal ſervices, the beſt liberty that can be given to peaſants is to compound all ſuch for money, which makes their burthens regular, however heavy they may be; and when this ſyſtem is extended as far as it will go, it includes the tenures of land; ſo that all the

eſtates

estates are let on lease, and the landlord's whole property pays him a regular interest in money: this is the highest advantage that can any where be made of the soil—it will in this case always be best cultivated, and yield a greater total product than in any other system, at the same time that many more people are maintained than in any other way. It is not at all necessary that a country should be free, in order for this system to reign; it is as general throughout France, and the arbitrary governments in Italy, as it is in England. The people, it is true, may be oppressed; but then the oppression is different: in France, the proportion of taxes paid by the farmers and peasants is quite out of all proportion to the other classes of the people; but then there is a regularity in their burthens, which renders them bearable. Taxes upon land, cattle, crops, or on whatever they may be laid, must in their nature have something of regularity and proportion in them; but the personal service in which the lower ranks of Poland are kept, is a mere slavery, such a despotism as the planters in the West-Indies use over their African slaves. Compared with this, the oppressed state of the Russian peasants is an absolute freedom; besides which,

which, there are many farmers who hire their lands by tenures.

The 21ſt carried me about forty miles to Elbing; the country all ſandy, yet tolerably well cultivated. It is remarkable that buckwheat, upon theſe ſands, very often yields as profitable a produce as wheat on the beſt ſoils: they get five or ſix quarters an acre off it; and the ſtraw they reckon excellent food for their cattle in winter. Swediſh turneps they alſo raiſe to advantage upon them; and tillage is ſo eaſy, from the lightneſs of the draught, that they plough their land, after the firſt time, with a ſingle horſe or cow: but this ploughing with cows is only while they are dry; they do not uſe them while they give milk. Elbing is, next to Dantzick, the moſt conſiderable town in Poliſh Pruſſia: it is a pretty, neat, and well-built place, with a trade that is ſufficient to give a briſk circulation of money among the inhabitants: they load many ſhips in a year, ſometimes above thirty ſail, with corn, timber, potatoes, and hides. It is always ſtriking, in every little town, to ſee the ſuperiority that reſults from trade: a ſmall commerce gives a circulation and a wealth, that diffuſes happineſs through every claſs of the people; the houſes are better built, new ones are erected, and every body

body lives well. But in a country town, supported by nothing but the agriculture around it; every thing is the contrary; the houses are poorly built, many are falling into ruin, and all ranks of the people are poor and unhappy. Such are the consequences of bringing commerce into a country, which never fails of giving a new appearance to every object.

The 22d I arrived at the famous city of Dantzick; the distance about forty miles. I crossed several branches of the Vistula, part of the country being within the liberties of the city. This territory, though a poor sandy soil, is most highly cultivated, and shews, in every acre, the infinite advantages which result from liberty and wealth. The burghers have their villas in this territory; and all of them have farms, which they manage in a manner much superior to the husbandry that is to be seen any where else in Poland. I saw some very fine fields of wheat on this apparently barren land, which I dare say the most fertile land in Poland does not exceed: this was owing to manure brought from Dantzick, such as dung of all sorts, ashes, the sweepings of the streets, the offals of the shops, &c. which being carried out of the city, unto heaps, is sold into the country by the public scavengers;

scavengers; most of it is bought by the Dantzickers for their farms; and they raise by this means as fine corn, &c. on their poor sand, as the richest soils yield that are not equally manured.

Dantzick is a very confiderable city, well situated on the mouth of the Vistula, with a very advantageous harbour for all but the largest ships. It very much resembles Hamburgh, both in the loftiness of the houses, the manner of building them, and in the narrowness of the streets. The streets and houses are much cleaner than any others in this part of the world; but neatness is not carried to the length it is in Holland. The principal streets are planted on each side in the Dutch way, which is an instance of ill taste in the original, which one cannot but be surprised at ever seeing copied. The city is not large, the circumference not exceeding three miles: it is fortified with a wall, and a double ditch; but the strength alone that is its security, is the interest of all their neighbours that the place should continue free: in which circumstance it is in the same predicament as Hamburgh. Two thousand regular troops, excellently provided and armed, would be a very weak garrison; but they have not seven hundred to spare, and those neither in discipline,

arms,

arms, or magazines, comparable to the same number of men in any regular service in Europe. In a word, Dantzick has a strength to resist nobody but the Poles. They have an arsenal full of useless arms, and talk of possessing two or three hundred pieces of cannon; but a great train of artillery may be as insignificant, as are these of Dantzick, as a magazine of match-locks.

But the commerce of this city is the object that is alone worth attention; it possessing, they reckon, sixteen in twenty parts of all the trade of Poland. This is by means of the river Vistula, and its numerous branches, which spread through a vast extent of that kingdom, and are navigable almost wherever they go. The great article of export is corn, and particularly wheat; they send off some years to the amount of five, six, and seven hundred thousand pounds; and once the amount arose to one million two hundred and forty thousand pounds. Of late years, the quantity is much declined, and, since the present troubles in Poland, has been very trifling; so that the total, last year, it was said, did not amount to one hundred thousand pounds. All the corn comes in sloops and flat-bottomed barges, that carry from thirty to sixty tons, and some more, and wholly on account of the landlords, who are all nobles by virtue of their poffeffing lands. It is raifed on their eftates by their peafants, who, as I before obferved, are all flaves; fo that the Poles may be faid to farm their whole eftates, whatever be the extent: the barges are their own generally, and the watermen that navigate them are fome of them their vaffals, and others freemen, whom they hire in the cities and towns on the river. It is fold to merchants at Dantzick, who lodge it in their granaries, which are more capacious than thofe of any town in Europe, fome of them eight ftories high. The boats bring, befides corn, all the other articles of fale which the Polifh eftates produce, particularly pot-afh, mafts, plank for fhip-building, pipe ftaves, which are better than thofe of Hamburgh, bees-wax in large quantities, fome hemp and flax, and formerly much of it manufactured into facking, packing-cloths, and even linen, but this of late years is much declined: of all thefe articles, to the amount of three or four hundred thoufand pounds, but fometimes not near fo much. The boats, on their return, carry back to the nobles, cities, and towns, all the commodities and manufactures which they want. Among thefe are reckoned, iron from Sweden, of which they once took two thoufand tons a year,

year, but the import is fallen to a thousand; East-India goods of all sorts, manufactures of woollen and fine linens, silks, brandy, wines, &c. The Dutch have all the supply of India goods, and most of that of linen and woollen; and the French the principal part of the silks, brandy, wines, and all the West-India commodities. As to England, her trade with Dantzick is very inconsiderable, which is entirely owing to our taking off very few of her commodities: we never pay money for what plank, pot-ash, or hemp we import; and when wheat is so dear in England, that foreign corn is admitted, our merchants have sometimes sent many ships thither to load with wheat, and have paid for their cargoes with our manufactures, of which none are so acceptable in Poland as the hardware goods of Birmingham, Sheffield, Rotherham, &c.

Making use of a letter of recommendation, which I had brought from the Count Selliern, to Mr. Pratsky, a very eminent merchant at Dantzick, and one whose great wealth shews how well he understands the trade of the city, gave me an opportunity not only of getting the preceding particulars upon better authority than I could otherwise have done, but, at the same time enabled me to make some enquiries concerning the present state of Poland, respecting the factious views and defigns of the feveral parties which at prefent harrafs that kingdom. I had for three years paft read much concerning them in the public prints of many countries, but could never clearly underftand the real ftate of the kingdom till I travelled from the Ukraine to Peterfburg. The account he gave me was this.

"Poland is divided into two grand parties, the Roman Catholicks, and the Proteftants and Greeks. The former, for fome ages paft, have omitted (as has been the cafe in every country of Europe) no opportunities of oppreffing the latter, and depriving them of that religious liberty to which they have a right by the conftitution of the kingdom. Thefe oppreffions and invafions of privileges begot confederacies of nobles, profeffing the Reformed or Greek religions, who entered into compacts for the defence of their faith, and declaring a full refufal to acknowledge any fovereignty, until their complaints were redreffed. This ftroke was copied immediately in moft parts of the kingdom where thofe religious are found. This gave rife to counter confederacies of the Roman Catholick nobles, with this addition, that they, in their agreement, declared all who did not accede to it to be enemies to the kingdom.

A

A civil war immediately commenced: Ruffian troops, which had long been in the kingdom, were greatly increafed, upon the Emprefs's declaring, in a general manifefto, her protection of the Greek and Reformed religion; and all parts of the kingdom were immediately in arms. In this war, the King, who difliked the whole of thefe proceedings, has been neuter; though it is very well known that the Ruffians are his friends, and that their power preferves him on the throne. The fuccefs of the war at firft was various; but every where the effect of it was deftroying and plundering each other's eftates, and utterly ruining a confiderable part of the kingdom. In the plunder taken on either fide, the peafants are always the moft valuable part: fuch as are not armed by their mafters, but remain at home to cultivate the land, are, upon a fkirmifh or incurfion which proves fuccefsful, carried off and planted upon the victors lands, where they are moft feverely treated, if they do not immediately conform to the religion of their new mafters. Such a fyftem of making war, which has now ravaged Poland three years with great violence, it may eafily be fuppofed, is well enough calculated for reducing the whole kingdom to the condition of a defart. The Ruffians have in

general

general been too hard for their enemies, and have cut in pieces a great number of their confederacies as faſt as they are formed; upon which occaſion the counter-reformed Poles enter and utterly deſtroy their eſtates, carrying off the peaſants, and fixing them upon their own lands; and many are ſent into Ruſſia from almoſt every expedition, which, of all the reſt, are thoſe only who have any chance of being fixed out of the reach of conſtant revolutions. This is the preſent ſtate of the kingdom: more than half of it has been laid waſte ſince the war began; and what threatens the whole is, the number of Roman Catholic confederacies, which are formed as faſt as the Ruſſians deſtroy the old ones. Nothing can bring any degree of peace to the kingdom, but the Empreſs increaſing her troops to ſuch a number, as to make a conqueſt of all the Roman Catholic part of the kingdom: and this would give umbrage, it is thought, to other powers, although ſome of them have declared in favour of the Reformed and Greek cauſe—that is, in favour of liberty of conſcience. While the preſent war laſts between Ruſſia and Turkey, the Empreſs cannot ſpare either troops or money for ſuch a plan; but if a peace is concluded with the Porte,

we

we may then look for more decisive measures."

Upon my asking him his sentiments of the Russian acquisitions, and their keeping possession of so many provinces, driving away the Polish nobility from their estates, and carrying most of the peasants into Russia; intimating, that I thought the Empress had a fair chance of acquiring something important; he replied,—" I do not apprehend that the Empress of Russia will think of seizing any Polish provinces, because that would make not only all moderate persons, and all well-wishers to their country among the Poles, her implacable enemies, but would deprive her of the strongest pretence she has of interfering, and thereby governing Poland: at the same time, it would bring her into a war with Prussia and Austria; for neither of those powers would see such Russian acquisitions, and sit by quietly. The aims of that princess, which I have little doubt are those of a true politician, are to support the party of her own religion, and prevent their being oppressed, and to gain such a general power in the kingdom, as to have her will be treated, in all great national measures, with due respect. Her carrying away the Polish peasants to people her crown lands is most

certainly

certainly a very political conduct; for she will add thereby equally to her strength and wealth."

M. Pratſky inſiſted on my taking a dinner with him, which I did. He has a large and convenient houſe, well furniſhed, and much in the Engliſh manner. His wife is an agreeable, ſenſible woman, a native of Sileſia, who talked politicks inceſſantly, and was a ſtrenuous advocate for the King of Pruſſia. They had a beautiful young lady, their daughter, who entertained me on the harpſichord; Dantzick being pretty well ſupplied with muſicians from Germany. M. Pratſky lives elegantly, but in the German manner, which is all the taſte there: they ſit long at meals, and drink very heartily: and among all the nations that are fond of the pleaſures of the table, there is always much ſociety, and a deſire of pleaſing, which does inſtead of the more refined manners of the ſouthern countries. Miſs Pratſky, and other ladies I ſaw, aim in their dreſs, I obſerved, at an imitation of the French taſte: but I cannot ſay I could ever admire any imitations, even in dreſs: whatever nation affects to follow the taſte of another, will never make any other figure than that of an halting copyer, who ſhews as much aukwardneſs as faſhion. The Engliſh

never

never make such fools of themselves as when they copy the French in their dress; the two nations are of different genius, and different manners; we never come up to the extravagance of the original; our copy is always tame: go from London to Paris, you are in a new world; you find what was called French, to be a miserable defective copy of a miserable original.

During my stay at Dantzick, I was at the Golden Crown, a very good inn lately fitted up and kept by a Dutchman; he charges very reasonably, and supplied me with good fish very fresh, and his wines are excellent, particularly old hock.

The 26th I left Dantzick and took the road for Warsaw, in the province of Plofcow: I was informed there were several parties of confederates and much skirmishing, I therefore took the advantage of travelling with a Dantzick burgomaster, going on publick business to the King with a company of soldiers for his guard. That day we travelled above forty miles to Kirchow, a small town through a sandy track of country, but with many villages in it. The next day we got to Culm, once a famous place and a hanse-town, but it has long been in decay, and is now, though a large place, filled with nothing but beggars

and

and ruins. The situation is upon a hill, and would if the town was well built, be very pleasant. From hence we passed the 28th through Thorn to Wladiflaw; the former of these towns was a hanse, and a noted place for trade before that of Dantzick, but most of its commerce, and inhabitants are gone; it has still, however, a good appearance, the streets are broad, strait, and some of them well paved, and the houses large and handsome: here is yet some trade by means of the Vistula, which is what keeps the place from the ruin into which so many others have fallen. The country we passed is not sandy, but seems to be a good loam, and the appearance of the corn indictates good husbandry, but many estates are quite desolate; we went through three villages that had been reduced to ashes more than a year ago, and no signs yet of being rebuilt. Wladiflaw is a pretty well built town also on the Vistula; the only buildings in it that are of any note is the Cathedral; it being the see of a bishop, an old Gothic edifice, and the bishop's palace, which has been much damaged by a siege the town stood.

The 29th we went 30 miles to Plockskow, on the banks of the river, except where marshes prevent; the surrounding country is a very rich soil, and not having suffered from

an

an enemy, shewed many signs of good cultivation: great champain tracks of open country are covered with wheat, which looked very well: the ploughs were busy in preparing for barley—no oats are cultivated here. The land seemed very well tilled by a couple of little horses and two oxen: but the ploughs are of a most aukward construction, and the peasants know not how to turn a straight furrow; they go as crooked as can well be imagined, which is disagreeable to look at, tho' I apprehend not the worse for the corn. They sow a good deal of hemp and flax in this neighbourhood, which they are very well situated for sending, with their corn to Dantzick. Wheat produces two quarters an acre; barley three, and pease two and an half. An acre of hemp, or of flax is worth about fifty shillings. They have large herds of cattle, which they feed in summer in the marshes on the Vistula; and in winter upon cabbages and turneps, which they always boil in the German manner before they give them to the cattle: this is not of much consequence where wood is so plentiful; but in England would do only in the neighbourhood of coal mines. But it is highly worthy of trial, to see how it would answer to follow this custom; because, if one acre boiled goes as far as three or four raw, which I have heard it does, there are many situations in which it would be very adviseable. We passed near a nobleman's mansion, surrounded by a double moat—full of water, and some cannon mounted on the battlements; my fellow-traveller told me, that this castle had been often besieged by the opposite party; but the nobleman driving all his peasants and cattle immediately in, had yet been successful in repelling them, which seems to be the only system of life in Poland for any person to have the least security; but of late he has had the fortune to escape any ravages, and is remarkable for the industry and attention with which he cultivates his estate, and takes a most fatherly care of all the peasants on it. This is a very rare instance in Poland; for they are generally used, as I have often observed, in a most oppressive manner; but the good effect of this contrary treatment is extremely visible in the case of this nobleman, who, tho' with only a small estate compared with many in the kingdom, has by means of a regular and consistent conduct towards his vassals, and by a constant attention to the culture of his land been able to save much money, part of which he has laid out in fortifying his castle, which has more than once preserved his property and his peasants,

and

and the reſt is lodged in the bank of Dantzick.

The 30th we reached Zadrzin, which is a ſtage of more than forty miles, through a very fine rich country, part of which is fully cultivated: They ſow very large quantities of wheat and barley, but no rye, or oats, peaſe or beans; they fallow their lands for wheat, and alſo lay all their dung in for it, and afterwards take two ſucceſſive crops of barley; ploughing thrice for each. Wheat yields four quarters an acre, and barley three. They alſo ſow ſome hemp and flax, and get as fine crops as any in Poland. The country is divided into four eſtates, and has eſcaped being plundered, which is owing I ſuppoſe, to the vicinity of the capital, where there has generally been a pretty ſtrong garriſon. All this country on the Viſtula, and between Dantzick and Warſaw, is the beſt ſituated of any in Poland; for the voyage to the former city is ſhort, and there are many populous and conſiderable towns, particularly Warſaw, which take off large quantities of the products at a good market, which is an advantage of the moſt valuable kind.

From Zadrzin is only forty miles to Warſaw, the road running all the way within ſight of the Viſtula; in ſome places ſkirting marſhes, but in others all through an arable country. This we travelled the 1ft of May, arriving at that city in the afternoon. It is the feat of government, the capital of the kingdom, and the refidence of the King; yet there is nothing ftriking in it. The ftreets are many of them crooked and ill paved, the buildings have little of elegance in them, tho' fome new ones, few in number make a tolerable fhew; thefe are houfes belonging to the Polifh nobles, who make Warfaw their winter refidence. The royal palace is a noble edifice, being beyond comparifon the fineft building in Poland. The apartments are very fpacious, and fome of them new fitted up and furnifhed in the Englifh manner, being executed by London artifts, brought from thence at the king's expence: The room they call the Hall of Victory, from formerly having been a hall, is converted into a faloon hung with tapiftry from Bruffels; the ceiling, panels, door-cafes, and window frames all neatly executed in white carving gilt: The rooms are very numerous, and all the offices for a court extremely convenient. And here let me obferve, that notwithftanding the prefent troubles which diftract the kingdom, yet there is a magnificence and a brilliancy difplayed around the King of Poland, which

fuits

suits very ill with the state of his mind, than which by all accounts nothing can be more unhappy. His majesty is certainly a man of quick parts, and has a truly patriotick concern for the miseries of his kingdom, which he is utterly unable to prevent: the state in which he lives is the regular court, which the republick maintains for all its kings; and it is so much a piece of republican magnificence, that the King has not all the offices in it in his own power. The court days do not exhibit any great circle of Polish lords—the most considerable in the kingdom are not only in opposition to the crown, but even in open arms against it. But the officers who are obliged to attend the nobles of the King's party, foreign ministers, and Russian officers, all together fill the room pretty well. There is a Polish regiment of guards, of a thousand men, disciplined in the Prussian manner, raised by the present King, and he often reviews them; the officers as well as private men are Poles, but none of them nobles; they are collected from all the other classes, and depend absolutely on the will of the King; this is a measure which was brought about by degrees, and with great art: it has been of uncommon consequence to the King; for by means of this body of troops, he has been able to move into several parts of the kingdom, without the guard of a Ruſſian army, which is a moſt unpopular, tho' a very neceſſary meaſure at preſent; on moſt occaſions it is not clearly known from what fund the King is able to pay this regiment, tho' his œconomy and private fortune would in better times eaſily accompliſh it; but the publick revenue in the midſt of the preſent confuſions, ſuffers extremely. If he is able to augment this corps by degrees, introducing none but men of low birth, mere ſoldiers of fortune, and abſolutely dependent on him; it may in time be a means of giving him an authority, which no other meaſure will ever bring about, for Poland will never ſee times of tolerable order, till her kings have abundantly more power than at preſent, and nothing but force will ever give them that power.

The fortifications of Warſaw, are ſufficient to prevent the town being inſulted by flying parties, or ſmall armies, but could not ſtand a ſiege of any duration againſt an army well provided; it has two good walls, flanked by many baſtions and tolerably lined with artillery; the ditch is broad and deep, and the waters of the Viſtula may be let into it at pleaſure. But the extent of theſe fortifications is too great to be defended effectually

with

with lefs than eight thoufand men. Warfaw is populous; being the capital of Poland, always brought great numbers to fettle in it, which the miferable ftate of moft of the other towns in the kingdom has lately increafed very much, fo that the number of its inhabitants are computed to be above eighty thoufand. There are at prefent in it many Polifh families, once in affluence, but now reduced to live in a very mean way: I am told that feveral cities in the Queen of Hungary's, and King of Pruffia's dominions are alfo full of them; Dantzick and Koningfburg, I know are. To what a fhocking ftate is this fine country reduced! wholly by the furious zeal of Roman-catholick bifhops, who would never be fatisfied without the total deftruction of the Proteftants and Greeks.

Upon our journey from Dantzick, we met with a fmall party that attacked us, and were more than once in fight of a band of robbers, who would have deftroyed us, had we been lefs guarded. This determined me in the journey I propofed making to Breflaw, to wait till I could go in fome company that would be a protection. Fortunately this offered in a week, by the Dutch refident returning home by the route of Breflaw; he had a party of Ruffian foldiers for his protection, and I was informed that I should lay in plenty of provisions and wine for our journey, as we should pass through a country that was nine parts in ten destroyed. The 7th of May we set out, and reached Rava the 9th; the distance about threescore miles; the first five from Warsaw under cultivation, but all the rest one continued desart, and as pitiable a sight as could well be seen. This line of country was not long since well peopled, and as well cultivated as any in Poland, which I could see by the numerous ruins of villages, single cottages, and seats, some quite destroyed, others tumbling down, and many in ashes: the country had most of it been arable, but the plough had no longer any business here; all the territory presented one face of desolation, the fields over-run with weeds, and becoming grass, without any cattle to feed on them. Rava was once a pretty town, and well peopled; but it is now a heap of ruins: out of ten thousand people that once lived here, there does not remain above seventeen houses inhabited, and those by some miserable creatures, too old to fly from the misfortunes of their town.

From Rava to Sirad is one hundred miles; in which track of country, though it evidently has all been cultivated, we saw but three villages

lages inhabited; all the reft burnt, and the people gone: the inhabitants of thefe yet venture to till a fmall quantity of land: we faw a little wheat, and feveral ploughs turning in barley; but who will reap it, the feedfmen little know. It is aftonifhing that the country from Dantzick to Warfaw fhould efcape fo well, while this has fuffered fo feverely. I there faw many devaftations; but they are nothing, compared with the condition of thefe territories. Sirad was in arms both within and without the walls; we therefore made a detour to the left, and paffed it. From thence to the boundary of Silefia is about forty miles; all which is one continued fcene of ruin. This is a journey of near two hundred miles; and a more melancholy one can fcarcely be travelled. Moderately fpeaking, I do not believe there are five thoufand fouls left in the whole country, Sirad excepted, the ftate of which town we were acquainted with: you may every where trace the plough; fome fields wholly ploughed, others half, others juft begun, but all over-run with weeds and grafs; fome remains of corn on the ground that never was reaped: houfes, barns, ftables, and all buildings, either burnt down, or falling for want

of

of repairs. Imagination cannot paint any scene more dreadful. Those landlords only are tolerably off, who fled to Germany at the beginning of the troubles, and live in expectation of peace, when they may return to their estates; the property of them is left, and will, on a pacification, enable them to recover themselves. But others who, in their defence, or to save their buildings from fire, bought off their enemies, met their fate at last, and cannot return without the load of debts; so that new buildings and settlements will be impracticable to them. I was assured that there are some hundreds of estates in the kingdom at present without any owners existing, so many whole families having been destroyed.

Travels through Germany.

CHAPTER VIII.

Silefia — Breflaw — Journey to Berlin — The Country — Agriculture — Defcription of Berlin — Prefent State of the King of Pruffia's Forces, Revenues, &c. — Saxony — Leipfick — Drefden — State of the Electorate.

NOTHING could be more ftriking, than the different appearance of Silefia from that of Poland. We entered it the 13th, and found the country full of villages, half of which at leaft were peopled with Poles; the land all cultivated, and much of it extremely well; the houfes and cottages in good repair; with all the appearances of eafe and happinefs; which formed fuch a contraft to the wretchednefs we had fo lately feen, that the view had the effect of making Silefia appear a paradife. Much of this muft certainly be occafioned by the great increafe of population from fuch numbers of Poles, who fly to efcape the miferies that every where defolate and lay wafte their own country. The King of Pruffia has officers appointed along all his frontiers, to fee that all thefe poor people are received, and to provide cottages for them as faft as poffible. In this work

work the King is at no expence; he only grants them permission to build cottages on any wastes or commons that are not absolute property; and his edict directs, that every neighbourhood should give all due assistance to the new settlers, and find them employment in husbandry or manufactures, after the rate of the country; and for the maintenance of such as do not find employment, he directs a tax to be laid on the district; but this cannot be lasting, as they have portions of land assigned them sufficient for their maintenance when brought into culture. Upon the wastes belonging to the crown, these portions are considerable enough to form, when cultivated, small farms, that hereafter will yield the crown a good rent. I saw many of these poor people, and it is hardly credible how much they seemed to enjoy themselves, on escaping the miseries of Poland, and finding such an humane protection in the territories of the neighbouring princes. I am informed that the Empress Queen receives them in the same manner in Moravia, Austria, and Hungary; many of them are in Transilvania. All the King of Prussia's long line of frontier, from the bottom of Silesia to Livonia, is open to them; and great numbers take refuge in every part of it. I before gave an account of the multitudes, to whom the Emprefs of Ruffia gave protection; if all this is considered, it muft at once be apparent, that the kingdom of Poland muft be amazingly depopulated, since it cannot be doubted but several millions of people, probably not lefs than three or four, are driven out of the country, or killed. Such a depopulation will take several ages to recover: and ftill this evil continues, without any appearance of its coming to an end; so that what the event will be, except leaving that country a mere defart, is very difficult to know.

We travelled thirty miles before we reached Breflaw. All this line of country is rich either in corn, meadow, or wood; the arable lands feemed very well cultivated; the wheat looked well, and the quantity of land occupied with it is confiderable: they alfo cultivate rye: the barley was all coming up, and feemed to promife good crops: they do not fow any oats; but they cultivate many cabbages as winter food for their cattle, and they reckon them much better, and to laft longer than turneps: potatoes they plant in large quantities for Breflaw, which city confumes a great deal of all the products of the earth; a vaft advantage to all the neighbouring country: the fmall potatoes they fatten their hogs

hogs with. The river Oder is navigable there, which is another great benefit to the country, always keeping the markets brisk, which of all other circumstances is the most certain means of introducing good husbandry. The ease and happiness of the peasants in this country is the more surprizing, as their taxes are very heavy, and carry as much into the King's coffers almost as into their own pockets. It can be attributed only to the regularity of his Prussian majesty's government; for that monarch looks so much into all his affairs, that there is no such thing in his dominions as irregular oppression: no minister, no officer dares to lay the hand of power on the defenceless poor; the King is their protector, and they had better be heavily taxed by him, than pay less, but be open with it to those numerous and accidental oppressions common in all other arbitrary governments.

Breslaw is a very extensive and well-built city: it is most advantageously situated on the Oder, upon the banks of which are some very fine streets; they are strait, well paved, and with many very well-built houses. There are several squares in it, and many public buildings, worthy the attention of a traveller; among which are several churches, the Jesuits college, the town-house, the arsenal, the

quay,

quay, &c. It is a bishop's fee, but the cathedral has nothing remarkable in it: also the seat of an university, which has for some time been in a flourishing situation. It was pretty strongly fortified in the last war; has a good wall, a double ditch, several bastions and ravelins, and a strong citadel; but the works are so extensive, that they require an army to defend them. The King keeps a garrison here of ten thousand men; they are drawn up in the great square every day, and go through their exercises, being as well-disciplined regiments as any in the King's service. There certainly results from this strong garrison, and the others throughout Silesia, which are all proportionably numerous, great security; of which the last war was a very striking proof; for, undoubtedly, the King owed his preservation to the excellent order all his fortresses were in, and the numerous garrisons they were furnished with: had the Austrians met him unprepared, they would have at least wrested Silesia from him, and perhaps have made some impression upon his hereditary dominions. There are many churches and convents in the city; but I did not hear of any thing in them that was particularly worthy of attention. There is a great trade carried on here by means of the Oder, and especially since the canal was cut between that and the Elbe, which communicates with Hamburgh. The articles in which this commerce is particularly carried on, are linen and flax, corn, timber, plank, &c. all which are staple commodities in Silesia, and produced in very great plenty. Most of the staves which form so great an export at Hamburgh, come from this duchy; and the quantity of oak timber and plank, which is exported from it, is very considerable. Upon all these articles the King lays a duty on the exportation; which is a piece of wrong politics of so flagrant a nature, that would make one think his abilities those of a warrior alone. The trade of Breslaw has declined a little since the troubles broke out in Poland; for in times of tranquillity in that kingdom, this province exports large quantities of goods thither, particularly linens, of which the Poles buy more than any other nation; but since the commencement of the civil war, they have been too much impoverished to be able to purchase any quantity worth mentioning.

The manufacture of linen in Silesia is very considerable: it employs many thousands of people, enriches the whole duchy, and brings in a very considerable revenue to the King.

Most of the linens which are bleached at Haerlam in Holland, and afterwards are so well known under the name of *Dutch*, are made in Silesia: formerly immense quantities were consumed in England; but since the great success which has attended the fabricks of Ireland and Scotland, this impolitic importation is come to nothing, and thereby vast sums saved to Great-Britain.——At this place I lessened my expences of travelling considerably, by paying off all my attendants, except my old Swiss, Martin, who has rode through the best part of Europe with me.

The 16th I left Breslaw, taking a post-chaise to Steinau, on the Oder; the distance thirty miles. This line of country is remarkably fine, fully cultivated, and in general well peopled. Landed property here is much divided; here and there is found an old baron's estate of great extent, around an old castle with all the marks of antiquity and grandeur; but in general the lands belong to persons enriched by trade and manufactures, which has had one excellent effect, that of diffusing much more liberty among the peasants than they have in other parts. Upon these estates, the lands are let in farms, as in England, and the peasants, not being vassals to tenants, are

hired

hired in the manner of our day-labourers, which is the fyftem of all others the moft beneficial. A common rent, in their farms, is from feven to eleven fhillings an acre: wheat yields two quarters an acre; barley three; buck-wheat four: the flax grounds are all inclofed by ditches, and they reckon an acre that yields three pounds a very good one. They keep all their cattle in winter in houfes, and feed them with boiled cabbages and ftraw. They lay moft of the manure they make upon their cabbage grounds, in the culture of which plant they feem to be very attentive. They make great ufe of mud from the Oder as a manure, and value it fo much, that they go feveral miles for it. They plough their land with oxen; the ftructure of their ploughs is remarkable; they feem, from the height of the wheels, to be very well in-ftructed in the doctrine of the lever.

The 17th I reached Grumberg, through forty-five miles of very indifferent road; dining at Glogau, a pretty town, agreeably fituated on the Oder, very ftrongly fortified, and always garrifoned with two thoufand men. It was anciently the refidence of the dukes of Glogau, and there are remains of their palace in the caftle. The cathedral is a very ancient and a fine building. They have some linen fabricks, and a good trade on the Oder. The country around it, and quite to Grumberg, is various, consisting of woods, arable, meadow, some waste, and also some marsh land. The villages are not very thick, and the peasants do not seem to be so well off as those nearer to Breslaw; what the reason is, I could not discover.

My next day's journey was thirty miles, through Crossen, to Frankfort on the Oder. Crossen is the capital of a territory of the same name: it is a very well-built town, having been rebuilt after a great fire which happened at the beginning of this century: the streets are strait, broad, and well paved: it is adorned with an handsome town-house, and five churches, one of which makes a good figure, being situated in the middle of a square.

Frankfort is in Brandenburg, and was once one of the most considerable cities in the Empire, being an hanse town, and an Imperial city; but it has lost most of its privileges. It is divided into the old and new town by the Oder, over which there is a handsome bridge, instead of an old wooden one which was burnt in the last war. The streets

streets are handsome, and many of the houses make a good figure, especially those which have been built since the last war. Their trade is considerable, both with Berlin, Hamburgh, the Baltic, and all Silesia; and before the war raged in Poland, with that kingdom also; so that it is one of the richest places in the King's dominions. They have an university, but it is not very well stocked with students of any consequence, though they have two well-built colleges. The town-house is an handsome building; and the arsenal is large and well filled. The most agreeable part of the town is the great market-place, which is surrounded by the best houses in the place.

The soil around Frankfort is sandy, and not very well inhabited: there is much waste land, which might be cultivated to good profit, considering the near neighbourhood of so many navigations, but encouragement seems to be wanting. I made many enquiries concerning the depredations of the Russians here; and from the information I could get, I have reason to believe that the accounts we had in England were much exaggerated: they burnt some villages, and raised heavy contributions; but as to utterly destroying a whole track of country,

country, it was not true. Another circumstance I should remark, which is, the mischief being all repaired which they did; for I have yet seen no signs of any of that ruin which fell from their hands: this is to be attributed to the good conduct of the King of Prussia, who, notwithstanding the general severity of his government, very wisely favoured those parts of his dominions that suffered most by war, as soon as the peace was made.

The 18th carried me 36 miles to Berlin; through a continued track of sand, yet tolerably cultivated in some parts, but much of it a dreary waste, and very thinly peopled. They find that the only very profitable crop upon these sands is buck-wheat, which they sow in large quantities, and they get a product which equals the best soils applied to that grain: when a piece of land has been more carefully managed than ordinary, it will yield a good crop of rye; but as to wheat or barley, it is hardly to be seen.

As I designed to make some stay at Berlin, I hired private lodgings; of which I had as good for fifteen shillings a week, as would have cost me five and thirty at London. But this city is not peopled proportionably to its size;

size; hence the general remark, that grass is seen in the streets, which is, however, only in one neglected quarter of the town; the other parts are very well built; the streets are remarkably spacious, long, and well paved; and the buildings in general are such as certainly rank it among the finest cities in Europe. Of the public edifices, those which are usually visited by travellers are, the royal palace—the arsenal—the churches of Notre Dame, St. Nicholas, St. Martin, and the Romish chapel —the theatre—the equestrian statue of Frederick the first, &c. The palace is a magnificent but an unequal building, like all those that are raised at different times: some of the apartments are large, and well proportioned; but they by no means answered my expectations, either in dimensions, fitting up, or furniture. The immensity of silver remarked by Mr. Hanway, when he was here, was all melted in the late war, and very little of it is restored. Much of the furniture, for a royal palace, is very mean; but this we are not to be surprized at, as the King gives his attention to so much greater objects. Some of the pictures are fine. The front of the arsenal would be very beautiful, but, as the above-mentioned traveller justly observes, it is profusely

loaded

loaded with ornaments. I viewed the contents, and was much entertained with them; for, very contrary to what is seen in moſt other buildings under this name, here are no uſeleſs arms, nothing but what is ready for immediate ſervice. The train is a very fine one. The theatre is in a moſt grand ſtile, admirably contrived to give much magnificence to the repreſentation of operas. A very few circumſtances excepted, it deſerves to be conſidered as a model for theſe buildings. The Romiſh chapel is a monſter of diſproportion, but the portico is elegant. The equeſtrian ſtatue of Frederick the Firſt is a fine performance; the horſe is remarkably fine, and there is much ſpirit in the attitude of the figure.

The fortifications of Berlin are regular; but the city is of too great extent to have any thing of ſtrength, if attacked by a powerful army. The number of inhabitants are reckoned at about an hundred thouſand. There is always a garriſon of from eight to twelve thouſand men in it. Charlottenburgh is a ſmall palace within a mile of Berlin; the rooms of which are ſmall, but very elegant: it contains nothing that appears very ſtriking to a traveller; the ball-room is handſome,

but

but much exceeded by many others. The gardens here, as well as at Potſdam, have nothing in them but regularity, which is diſguſting. Sans Souci is a detached apartment in a garden; but nothing of this ſort that I have ſeen abroad, is comparable to a number of places we have in England: nor do I think any of theſe palaces and boxes in the neighbourhood of Berlin are tolerable in taſte: the only natural beauty they had was the river, and that is moulded into a canal for them: they have no verdure; the walks are ſand, and the ſituations in general flats.

There is a good deal of commerce carried on at Berlin, by means of the canals which join the Spree and the Oder, and the Oder and the Elbe; by which means there is a moſt advantageous communication with Hamburgh, the Baltick, and all Sileſia. This is of great conſequence to the manufactures of Berlin, which are numerous and flouriſhing: they have fabricks of ſilk, ſtuffs, woollen cloths of ſeveral ſorts, and in particular one which clothes moſt of the army; tapeſtry, laces, glaſs, a little hardware, &c. The King gives great encouragement to all manufactures, which has had a great effect in a place where he found many fabricks fixed by French
refugees

refugees after the revocation of the edict of Nantes, whose posterity now carry on the principal trade of the city. Berlin supplies Silesia with great quantities of these goods; and before the civil war raged in Poland, that kingdom took off much. They have a small export to the Baltic; formerly to Sweden, but that is now no more.

I was twice or thrice at court, more to see the King, than for any other entertainment. I saw him about nine years ago, and was much surprized to find him so little altered. The immensity of fatigue, both of body and mind, which he went through during the last war, one would have apprehended must have entirely broke him; but he has, by a regular way of life, and great abstemiousness, both then and since, prevented any ill effects. Bodily fatigue may be physick, and mental labour not very destructive, but anxiety is the destroyer, against which it is very difficult to guard: for several years the King was uncertain of his fate; victories had little effect, defeats were ruinous, and he could scarcely conjecture whether he was to be stripped of several provinces, or even his whole dominions. In such a situation, we may easily conceive that anxiety must commit great ravages on
him;

him; and I muſt own myſelf ſurprized to ſee his health continue ſo good. His principal amuſement is exerciſing his troops; to ſee them, is one of the moſt entertaining ſights at Berlin. It is thought that the King himſelf has not ſo nice an eye as formerly to the *minutiæ* of the tactic, but his officers keep it up in the higheſt perfection. His army is at preſent more numerous, and better provided than ever; they do not fall ſhort of one hundred and forty thouſand men; and there is not a regiment in his ſervice that is not ready for marching: his whole army, artillery, baggage, and all attendants, could be in the field upon a week's notice at any time; his fortreſſes are all in better order than before the laſt war, and ſome places made of great ſtrength upon the frontiers of Sileſia, which never before were fortified at all. His treaſure is reported to be conſiderable, and he certainly is not encumbered with debts; for the laſt war, immenſe as it was to him, did not make him contract a ſhilling of debt, tho' it is certain his antagoniſt, the Queen of Hungary, anticipated many of her revenues. If all things are conſidered, it will appear very evident, that his power is better eſtabliſhed than ever, and that he has no proſpect

of

of seeing another confederacy, which will bear so hard upon him as the last. Austria will not be eager to attack him, after having failed, with every possible advantage on her side. If she could not wrest Silesia from him, when France, Russia, Sweden, and Saxony were in alliance with her, and their power so actually brought to bear upon him, that he fought battles with them all; such a confederacy is not to be looked for in an age; and if it failed in its aim, that aim may be pronounced impracticable. Saxony, it cannot be expected will unite again, unless it be with Prussia, but the situation of it considered, if it proves an enemy, it will be an enemy swallowed up as in the last war, and the country made to contribute amply to pay the expence of it. Russia will scarcely unite against the King, with whom she is now in close alliance; it would be extremely contrary to her interest. France will always be found in full employment by England; she will not quickly send armies against Prussia. The King therefore has the satisfaction of enjoying peace.

These are the ideas of the Berlin politicians, who all declare the peace will be lasting, from the great jealousy of Austria, and Russia, either opposing or uniting with each other:

other: every party is strongly armed, and looks on in silence, except Russia, who, knowing her own strength and fearless of consequences, carries on a most extensive war with Turkey and in Poland.

The King's revenues amount at present, to about a million and an half sterling; a sum which in England appears small; but if the different value of money there, and in Brandenburg be considered; and likewise, the uncommon exertions of œconomy unequalled in any other court; this sum, I am confident, is in the King's hands as good as four millions, perhaps as five in England. The land-tax throughout his dominions is regular, and equals about nine shillings in the pound: the crown lands yield a considerable rent, and are as well managed to profit, as a private gentleman's estate. The customs are but a small article; they are gathered in his ports on the Baltick and at Embden. The excise is general on all the necessaries of life, and rises so high as forty per cent. These taxes are very heavy; but such is the regularity of his government, and so little oppression is met with from ministers and revenue-officers, that the people are beyond comparison happier than in the dominions of Saxony, Austria,

stria, or Bavaria. Much of his succefs in the late war, was doubtlefs owing to the subsidy he received from England: the difcontinuance of which, and the breaking off all connections between the two courts, struck hard upon him; for it took him out of the hands of France, from whom he received a subsidy of three hundred thoufand pounds a year, and left him without an equivalent from England. The treatment he received from the latter country, upon the change of that miniftry which had conducted the war, made an impreffion upon him much againft England, of whom he has often expreffed himfelf with fome acrimony: what the refult will be in future political arrangements, is not eafy to fay; but if the connection continues between France and Auftria, that between England and Pruffia, muft in the nature of things be renewed; for when one part of Europe throws itfelf into an alliance offenfive to the reft— a counter alliance muft ever be formed, or all good ideas of politicks be abfolutely given up.

The 1ft of June I left Berlin, and got to Britzen, the diftance thirty miles: all which track of country is very fandy, though tolerably populous, and fome of it well cultivated.

tivated. They sow much buck-wheat; and were now ploughing for turneps, which they sow the middle of this month: and I believe this root and buck-wheat, with a very little rye, to be all the products these poor sands yield, and yet they seem to be very well manured; for the countrymen house their cattle in winter, and raise by that means large quantities of dung, which they mix with a kind of stiff earth, which they dig from under the sand; a compost which I should suppose, must agree extremely well with such dry barren soils.

The 2d I advanced no further than Wittenburg, the distance only 15 miles. In this journey I passed from Brandenburg to Saxony, and the soil changes almost immediately for the better, and the population of the country also. The soil is a good loam, which yields tolerable crops of wheat; they have also barley, and I remarked a few pieces of flax. Wittenburg was noted before the last war for its cloth manufactories, and for dying better than at any other place in the electorate; the latter business is yet found here, though not near so much as formerly; but most of its fabricks are removed to Berlin, so that the

place

place has not been able to recover the ruin it met with in the war. Martin Luther's church is yet standing, tho' three hundred years old, and has seen so many sieges, cannonades, and bombardments without any damage.

The 3d I went to Leipsick, the distance 30 miles, through a country naturally exceedingly fertile, but carries many marks of the miseries of the late war. Most of it has been well cultivated, but upon riding into several fields now in grass, and whose appearance indicates wretched management, I found they had been arable ones within a few years; and upon making enquiries, I had several spots pointed out to me, whereon stood small villages, consisting of farm-houses, now no more; and all the lands which belonged to them, and once yielded abundant crops of corn, are now little better than waste and common forest land, whereon the tenants of the same landlord turn their cattle. This is not the case with two or three places, but continues for many miles; and is owing to the nobles to whom the country belongs, having ruined themselves with paying military contributions so often, that at last, they had nothing to pay when their buildings were burnt down, and themselves left too poor to erect new ones: This is generally the reason, why the seat of war is so very injurious to a country; for nothing is so great an evil, as land cultivated, formerly belonging to owners, too poor to raise the buildings necessary for bringing it again into culture. If the landlords of such a country would allow every thing to be destroyed the first campaign, they would be reduced it is true; but then they would be free from those enormous debts which not only carry their ruin with them to the graves of such as groan under them, but entail misery upon their children.

Leipsick, the suburbs included, is one of the most considerable cities in this part of Germany, notwithstanding its having suffered very severely in the two last wars, and felt some heavy strokes, which are not yet recovered. It has been the theatre of almost every war that has happened in Germany. In the famous one of thirty years, it was very often taken and retaken by the Swedes, and Imperialists; no less than five times in two years: It felt the weight of Charles XII's invasion of Saxony, than whom there have been few more brutal invaders. And the two last wars succeeded each other very quickly; its trade and buildings much declined in them.

them. The city itſelf is not an agreeable place, from the narrowneſs of the ſtreets, and the height of the houſes, which riſe to eight or nine ſtories; but the ſuburbs are much more ſpacious and better built; they are alſo pleaſant, from the number of areas, and gardens in them; and from the conflux of three ſmall rivers. They have not many publick buildings at Leipſick that much deſerve a ſtranger's attention; the beſt among them is St. Nicholas Church, which is a very fine edifice. The town-houſe is an old but a good ſtructure; the exchange is another: and around the great market place are many houſes of private merchants, which make an uncommon figure for buildings of that ſort; but there are ſeveral traders in the city, that have made conſiderable fortunes, and before the laſt war treble the number; but the greateſt among them upon the breaking out of it, removed themſelves and their effects to Hamburgh. The univerſity is one of the moſt famous in Germany, and much frequented by ſtudents of family and fortune; but this alſo declined much in the laſt war.

Trade is the ſoul of Leipſick: Conſidering that it is an inland place, and without the advantage even of a navigable river, the greatness of its commerce is very surprizing; but it is owing to its fairs, of which they have three very considerable ones every year. To them merchants bring or send goods of all sorts from every part of Europe: all the manufactures of Germany, France, Italy, England, Holland, and Flanders are met with here: Vast magazines are formed of East India goods of all sorts; of West India commodities; of wines, brandies, fruits, silk, hemp, flax, iron, and in a word all sorts of products: And purchasers resort hither from every part of Germany and the North. These fairs also carry off great quantities of the fabricks which are made at Leipsick, of which there are several sorts; such as silk, cotton and woollen manufactures, paper, gold, and silver laces, &c. but all these suffered much from the last war; nor have they recovered themselves to any thing like their former success: Indeed, I observed in conversation with several merchants here, that they had all a distrust that they were by no means secure from fresh visits of the Prussians; and while this is the case, (at which we cannot be surprized) it is not to be wondered that commerce and manufactures do not thrive. The injury the whole Electorate sustained fuſtained laſt war, in the deſtruction of its manufactures and trade; the ruin of its agriculture, and the decline of its population, was of an exceedingly great amount, and ſuch as cannot be recovered without the moſt unremitting attention, and political conduct of half a century; before which time it will probably ſee in ſome cauſe or other, a renewal of its calamities. If theſe circumſtances are conſidered, with the oppreſſive government of all the German princes that have an abſolute authority, we ſhall have reaſon to wonder at any trade at all being found in Saxony.

The 6th, I travelled thirty miles to Meiſſen, through the fineſt part of Saxony; and which, notwithſtanding the fury of the late war, is now a populous and a well cultivated country; there is a great deal of arable land, and very fine champain fields, covered with corn; many villages, and the people ſeemed to be active, and quite alive in their buſineſs. Part of the females were collected in ſmall knots in the villages ſpinning wool; others drove the horſes and oxen that drew the ploughs; this employment of the women is an excellent ſign, where the men do not, in conſequence, indulge in idleneſs, which is the caſe in ſome countries. They cultivate a great deal of wheat and barley, and were now ſowing ſome

buck-

buck-wheat; but it is a grain for which their lands are too good, the pooreſt ſands will rival them: They cultivate turneps, cabbages; and alſo cabbages for feeding themſelves and their cattle; their herds are numerous; they feed them not only in their meadows, but alſo upon clover, of which I ſaw ſeveral large pieces, a thing I had not remarked of a long time. I enquired into their management of it; they ſow it with barley, and in the ſucceeding year, either mow it twice for hay, thrice ſometimes; or elſe feed ſheep, young cattle, cows, oxen, and horſes upon it: the hay they prefer to meadow hay. They keep it two years upon the ground, and after that plough it up for any ſort of crop, but do not ſeem to conſider it as a peculiar preparation for wheat, which is the idea in England: It has not been long cultivated here, but ſpreads very faſt, from their finding the profit of it to be great. The lands here are cultivated by both the landlords and peaſants; the latter are in general farmers, and not of very little ſpots, but they are bound to apply a part of their time with their teams, &c. to cultivate thoſe parts of the eſtate, which the landlord holds in his own hands, and which are uſually pretty conſiderable.

Meiſſen

Meissen is a little town, weakly fortified, but with a strong castle on the Elbe; it is only remarkable (the Dresden Porcelane excepted) for a covered bridge of wood over that river; the cathedral I had been told was a fine building, with many fine electoral monuments in it, but I found it worthy of very little observation. The manufacture of Porcelane, was once more famous here, than at any other place in Europe, but the last war almost ruined it; upon the King of Prussia's irruption into Saxony, most of the workmen, and the materials were removed; but the war continuing so long, and Saxony remaining in the hands of the Prussians, some of the people died, and others were lost; some the King of Prussia secured, and sent them to Berlin; where he attempted to establish a similar manufactory, but he has executed nothing comparable to the old Dresden pieces. Upon the establishment of peace, the works at Meissen were restored, and a fresh set of workmen, with some old ones, resumed the manufactory: I have seen the best pieces they have made, and shall venture to assert, that the manufacture is lost; for they are not in the clearness of the white, to be compared with the metal formerly made; as to fine painting, it is any where to be had, and therefore

fore not peculiar to the Drefden ware. This is a great lofs to the curious, and lovers of fine Porcelane all over Europe; and the more fo, as none of the numerous fabricks fet up in England, France, or Holland, have come near equal to it.

The 17th I reached Drefden, which is only fifteen miles from Meiffen, through the moft beautiful line of country I have feen in Germany; it is all hill and dale, corn, vines, and meadows along the banks of the Elbe a continued picture; the river is every where feen to advantage, with the beautiful circumftance of the banks being high and woody; a more entertaining picturefque fcene can hardly be viewed.

Drefden I can eafily conceive, was before the deftruction of the fuburbs, one of the fineft cities in Europe; but the Pruffians have much reduced its beauty, by burning down a great part of the moft beautiful quarters of it. The old city is fortified in a regular manner; the baftions are of ftone; and there is a double ditch, but yet the ftrength of it is nothing, unlefs the garrifon be very numerous: The river Elbe divides it into two cities, the old and the new. The bridge over that river which is built of ftone, is reckoned the fineft in Germany; but no perfon who has

been

seen that at Westminster, will think there is either beauty or magnificence in it. It is five hundred and forty feet long, thirty six broad, and consists of nineteen arches. The electoral palace is not a very striking building for the beauties of architecture; but there are many very fine and spacious apartments in it very splendidly furnished; much of it done since the war; for some of the best furniture was ruined by the Prussians, and a vast number of curiosities carried off. The King it is supposed, did not design to touch any thing, and no commander keeps a more regular discipline, but in so long a war so full of events, and those remarkably severe; a place of curiosities, must necessarily fare but badly. The stables form a magnificent building, being very spacious, and were once filled with some of the finest horses in Germany, but many of the stalls are now unoccupied; indeed the revenues of the electorate suffered to so great a degree in the late war, that Dresden has ever since exhibited a very different appearance; the court is no longer what it was, and all those circumstances which flow from great revenues, have sunk proportionably to the decline, which the Saxon income has experienced. No court in Germany was so profuse; but there is an œconomy in it now, which

which promifes a much happier adminiftration of affairs than has been experienced in the two laft.

The Romifh chappel is one of the fineft edifices at Drefden; it is a well-proportioned and magnificent building; moft highly ornamented: It was built for the private ufe of the late King and his court.

The chamber of curiofities, have yet a great many very beautiful models, and toys, which cannot fail entertaining any traveller; and the collection which they call the Kunts-kammar, which is chiefly of natural rarities, equal to any thing that can be feen; but as the particulars of thefe things have been publifhed by more than one traveller, I fhall not fwell thefe pages with a recital of them. The gallery of pictures, is equal to moft that are to be feen in Italy; and are kept in admirable prefervation. The pieces by Correggio are to be equalled no where but in Parma. A very magnificent work, containing plates of all the pictures in this gallery, was publifhed at Drefden, under the direct infpection of the late King.

The Indian palace, of which feveral writers have given long accounts, is in my opinion a very filly affair; and by no means even elegant. Count Bruhl's famous palace fuffered

fered moſt ſeverely in the war, at which nobody was concerned, from the foundation of all his grandeur being laid in the miſeries of the Saxons; and from his being the principal plotter, and adviſer of that war, which ruined his maſter. The picture gallery is one of the fineſt rooms I have any where ſeen.

From the beſt accounts I could get while at Dreſden, the decline in all the affairs of conſequence throughout the government of Saxony, upon account of the late war, is much greater than has been thought by ſome authors who have written lately. Before the war, the revenues of the electorate, by means however of very great oppreſſion, amounted to a million and an half ſterling; but I was aſſured, that they do not at this day, although near ſeven years of peace have intervened, riſe to ſeven hundred thouſand pounds, and yet the government is burthened with a very heavy debt. Saxony, before the war, contained near two millions of people; it has not now much above one: In Dreſden were an hundred and ten thouſand people, but at preſent it would be difficult to find half the number; ſuch ſtrong marks of decline are not to be miſtaken, they ſhew the ſeverity of the late war, in the moſt ſtriking colours; and prove clearly

clearly that if it had continued much longer, the whole electorate would have been made a defart.

The prefent government conducts all things in a very fenfible and political manner; they find the wretched ftate of the country will admit of nothing but an œconomy which has not been practifed in this country for a long while; the people fee and know the publick diftrefs, and do not repine at the taxes they are forced to pay, as all did when the amount was fquandered by count Bruhl, and the King, in cloaths, toys, and gewgaws. Only fifteen thoufand regular troops are kept up, but they have five or fix thoufand militia regularly difciplined. This is certainly acting with prudence; for the whole country is fo impoverifhed, that if they raifed by taxes a revenue to do otherwife, it muft be by the ruin of the people. They muft have time not only to recruit their loffes, but alfo their numbers. The foil is in general fertile, and the Saxons are induftrious enough to bring it into culture, if they have time given them, without making even peace itfelf too burthenfome, by taxation, and without hurrying them into another war, which could not fail of being ruinous to the whole electorate. Some encouragement has been given to agriculture and

and manufactures since the peace; particularly by an exemption from taxes in certain cases wherein they would be extremely burthensome; but the essential foundation of tolerable cultivation, or activity in carrying on fabricks, is wanting, which is wealth, or at least easy circumstances in the undertakers; but this electorate, the Prussians exhausted to so great a degree, that they left scarcely any wealth in it; the lands are in the hands of nobility so reduced, that they can scarcely live; much less are able to carry on improvements in the manner requisite at present, for being effectual in reviving husbandry in their country; and when this is the case, such a renovation must be left to common causes, the increase of the people, and of industry among the lower classes, which is always of most slow operation.

The amazing difference of the event of the war to Brandenburg and Saxony, is striking. The latter is so ruined and exhausted, as to lye almost at the mercy of any invader; without people, trade, revenues, or forces, on a comparison with what all those articles were before the war: on the contrary, the King of Prussia is in possession of as great an income as ever; a finer army, than when he began the war: his dominions suffered indeed, but the wounds seem to have been but skin-deep: certainly his country was not made the seat of war in the manner he made that of the Elector of Saxony. The contrast indeed is so striking, that if ever a new war breaks out between Prussia and Austria, Saxony most undoubtedly will not join the latter.

The 12th I set out from Dresden, and got to Lentmeritz, in Bohemia, in two days, passing through Pirna, and by the famous castle of Koningstein. Pirna is a little place among the mountains, and Koningstein is a castle situated on the top of a rock, three hundred feet high, and half a mile in circumference. The way to it is so difficult, that a company is sufficient to defend it against an army. In it is a well, above sixteen hundred feet deep, which supplies the garrison with water. In the labyrinth of these rocks and mountains, the King of Prussia caught the Saxon army and made them prisoners. The country is in general very wild and romantic, and the views of the Elbe running through such a region of mountains extremely grotesque: There are some vineyards planted upon southern spots of these mountains, where the grapes ripen tolerably, but the wine is not drinkable to those who have been used to that which is good.

CHAP-

CHAPTER IX.

Journey acrofs Bohemia—Prague—Defcription of the country—The people—Nobility—Hufbandry--Manufactures--Moravia--Olmutz--Brinn—Journey to Vienna—Defcription of the capital.

LENTMERITZ is a fmall town in Bohemia, fituated on the river Elbe; it has fome fortifications, but none of any great ftrength : near this place the King of Pruffia gained a great victory over the Auftrians in the laft war. The neighbouring country was feveral times the feat of war, and fuffered much : part of the mifchiefs done, are not yet recovered; for there are feveral tracks of land belonging to a Bohemian nobleman, who refides at Vienna, which were once arable, but are now over-run with grafs and weeds, and ftill have by no means near a ftock of cattle proper for the land; and fome villages are of a very poor appearance with feveral houfes almoft burnt down, that have not yet been repaired. The country that is cultivated, does not feem to be managed in an able manner;

ner; and the peasants are much worse treated than they are in Saxony.

The 18th I reached Prague, the capital of Bohemia, and one of the largeſt cities in Europe. The country through which the road runs is various; much of it is of a fruitful ſoil, and tolerably cultivated in ſome parts, but there are in every track many marks of bad huſbandry and inattention, greatly owing I ſuppoſe to a want of induſtry, and partly to the oppreſſion which the peaſants experience: They have ſome tolerable crops of wheat, but I never ſaw worſe barley, or any corn more full of weeds; and they value it ſo little, that on various pieces of barley and peaſe I ſaw cattle feeding, which made me enquire if they were ſown with intention to be eat green; but that was not the caſe; it is a mere inſtance of ſtupid neglect. I obſerved one or two pieces of flax, which looked very well. The winter food of their cattle is principally the cabbage, turnep, and red cabbage, which they cultivate in large quantities. I ſaw ſeveral young plantations of them, but they do not ſeem to manage them well.

Prague is very well ſituated on the river Muldaw; it is divided into two cities by that river. The fortifications are regular, and
much

much superior to what they were before the last war; but the city is of so great an extant, that it requires an army to defend it. It suffered very much by the siege it stood in the beginning of the war against the King of Prussia, who cannonaded and bombarded it in so severe a manner, that not many buildings escaped; whole quarters were beat down, or burnt, and I was shewn several very large gardens and young orchards, which before that siege were entirely covered with houses, then destroyed, and the people are too poor to rebuild them in a place where there are yet more houses than are occupied: scarcely any of the publick buildings escaped damage at the same siege. The university is one of the most famous in Germany, and has a vast number of students; the people at Prague talk of five thousand; what they might be formerly I know not, but at present they are short of three thousand. In 1409, when John Huss was rector, it is a fact that there were thirty thousand students here. The Jesuits college is one of the finest buildings in the city, but it suffered by several unlucky cannon balls, and is not yet thoroughly repaired. The bridge, which joins the old and the new town, is fifteen hundred and eighty feet long, by thirty broad, and has seventeen arches, and is all of stone; it is a solid edifice, has nothing of elegance in it; and when a traveller hears that it was an hundred and fifty years a building, he will suppose it must have been in an age extremely poor, or been undertaken by a prince of little spirit. The finest edifices in the world are rarely those which were so long in raising. St. Peter's at Rome is an instance against me, but St. Paul's at London, and the bridge at Westminster, are strong ones in my favour, and many more might be quoted. The royal palace, and the cathedral, are very mean buildings that contain scarcely any thing worthy of notice. What at Prague are much the best worth seeing, are the palaces of the nobility; some of which are very noble edifices, that would make a great figure in the best built cities of Italy; several of them are of very great size, with most spacious apartments, and very magnificent furniture. Those of the princes Lobcowitz, and Ischarnan, and the counts Galas, Straka, Czaslaw, and Manstein, deserve particular attention; they contain many apartments that are worthy of sovereign princes, but the number of very good pictures is trifling.

Most of the Bohemian nobility, who are a numerous body, keep their residence in winter at Prague, and in summer on their estates.

None

None of them refort to Vienna, but fuch as are in office in the court, which is a very uncommon inftance. It is their prefence in this city that alone fupports it; for without their refort, and the garrifon, which is generally pretty numerous, the city would be a defart; being utterly deftitute of both trade and manufactures: the univerfity does fomething, but not much. All the lower claffes here are poor; the burghers are treated by the nobles very contemptuoufly, to a degree not common elfewhere; if the place was ever fo well fituated for trade, or manufacture, this would be a fure means of damping their progrefs.

The 16th I left Prague, and went to Nymburg, a fmall town twenty five miles diftant; the country various, but much of it pretty tolerably cultivated; rather better than the track to the north of Prague. The peafants are treated in a wretched manner; they have hovels of the worft fort to live in, little better than thofe in Weftphalia; being loofe ftones laid on one another for the walls, and the crevices filled with mud, and the covering fome ftrong poles, with turf fpread on them, and a hole at top in the middle is all the chimney that any of them have; adjoining is their barn, built of the fame materials, in which they ftow their little corn, and keep their cattle in winter; each cottage has a few acres of land around it, with a cow or two, and a miserable pair either of horses, or oxen for ploughing their land. In general, Sunday is the only day in the week which they are allowed for cultivating this land, in order to raise provisions for subsisting on the whole week; but in seed-time and harvest, their lords indulge them with another: When I speak therefore of the husbandry of the country, I do not mean of the peasants, nor of the farmers, for there is scarcely any such thing, but of the nobility, and other landlords, who all cultivate their own estates by means of their agents and stewards. The peasants in every respect resemble nearly those of Poland, than whom they are not favoured more.

At first sight it may appear, that landlords, who act upon this system, must make far more of their estates, than those who let them, in the English manner, to farmers, because here the profit of the farmer is consolidated with that of the landlord; but, from the repeated observations which I have often had occasion of making, I am convinced that the case is the very contrary. If any estate was only of such a size as to form a good farm, it would be very true; but estates are thus cultivated

tivated whose extent is from twenty to thirty thousand acres of cultivated land, either meadow, pasture, arable, sheep-walk, or woods, all in some culture or other, and a vast track arable. To be forced to cultivate such immense farms, they are obliged to have swarms of bailiffs and agents. In every place where a farm-house should be, is a bailiff's house, who manages a certain track of land. Thus the landlord is at the monstrous expence of stocking his whole estate, and running all the chances of that stock, and at the same time has to keep as many bailiffs as if they were farmers, and who all live out of the land before he has his clear profit, as much as if they were farmers; with this great distinction, that being merely servants, they have little interest in the success of their husbandry, and consequently the master suffers all the usual inconveniences of such a situation: his agents of all sorts cost him as much as farmers would make for themselves, supposing them honest; and if they turn out otherwise, a great deal more. Thus he gets none of the farmers profit, at the same time that he loses the interest of all the money employed in stocking, and the chances to which that stock is liable. From which state of the affair, I think it is very evident, how much

much more beneficial it is to let out an eftate to farmers, for them to find the ftock, cultivate the land, and employ the peafants, not only in mere profit of the year, but with a view to future improvements, which muft always be conducted with far more effect by the people who work for their own intereft, than by others who do it for a mafter, and a mafter perhaps who is always abfent, or, if prefent, who underftands nothing of the matter. What great improvements have been made in England by tenants, who enjoy the benefit during their leafe, and then pay a frefh rent to their landlords on account of thofe very improvements! In population alfo the prince would reap a very great benefit; for when men are working for themfelves, their induftry will be very different from that of fervants; and in proportion to the general induftry, muft population be: the peafants would likewife meet with lefs oppreffion, and confequently increafe more.

'They fow a good deal of wheat in this line of country; but their principal crop is barley. I obferved many plantations of hops in the warm vales, where the foil is rich and deep: it is a common culture in moft parts of Bohemia, I am told; and when the fpot chofen for a hop-garden is fuitable, they find it more

profitably

profitably applied than for any other crop. Beer is a very great article of trade throughout the kingdom, much being exported to all the surrounding countries; this makes barley and hops particularly advantageous. Saffron is another crop, which I saw now and then: they prefer a light, dry loam on a stratum of rock for it; they think it very profitable; an acre of good saffron is worth about three pounds here. Turneps and cabbages they have in large quantities for the winter support of their cattle: they prefer the latter in general: I saw many crops somewhat advanced in growth, but they do not seem to be attentive to keeping them free from weeds.

The 17th I reached Leutmyssel, at the distance of forty-five miles, passing through two or three pretty towns upon the banks of the Elbe. This country is more beautiful than the preceding, and of a richer soil; in some parts there are hills, but not so great as to be unprofitable land, while the vales form some very rich arable and meadow land; most of which is pretty well cultivated, under wheat, barley, and beans, which are much sown here: wheat yields from two, to two and an half quarter per acre; barley something more; beans four quarters; they choose for these their stiffest wet soils. They feed on their meadows large herds of cows and oxen; and keep many sheep, but do not manufacture the wool; most of it is sold to Silesia and Saxony, both of which are much more industrious countries: They work up however some of their own flax into the same sort of linnens, as are made in Silesia, which is an employment of the poor people in many of the little towns in this kingdom; their earnings at this work are very small; a weaver in Silesia will earn about three and sixpence a week; but in Bohemia not more than half a crown: But provisions of all sorts are very cheap in both these countries. I saw two or three country seats belonging to noblemen; they are all built in the castle form, with a moat round, and seem to be extremely spacious; a nobleman of great fortune in this country, has seldom less than two or three hundred servants about him, when at his castle in the country; and he is an absolute monarch upon his estate, with power over every thing but life and death, and the royal revenue officers. This kind of dominion over all the lower classes, flatters the vanity and pride of the great, more than the amount of the advantages they would gain by the peasants being free; it is like the contrast of absolute authority to the limited power possessed by some kings; the latter

makes

makes their people happy and rich, and might have the fame effect upon themfelves, but they are all hunting after the former.

The 18th I got to Olmutz, the capital of Moravia, the diftance forty miles; croffing the mountains which feparate the two countries, thefe are not very lofty, nor craggy, but they fill a track of country, of feveral miles broad; they exhibit a wild territory, but little of which is cultivated: The peafants that inhabit thefe hills, are a rough intractable fet of men, that will not fubmit to the oppreffions under which their brethren of the plains groan; they have been often in rebellion, not againft the fovereign, but the lords to whom they are vaffals; they are in many refpects treated much better; and their houfes and little farms make a much better appearance; they have more and better cattle; fome of them are in poffeffion of fmall pieces of land which they have purchafed, and all are extremely tenacious of this kind of property; they do not work for their mafters more than three days in a week. It is always to be remarked, that the gradations of freedom are ever to be found in mountainous countries; in general fuch are free; but even under abfolute monarchs they enjoy more liberty, than the fubjects of the fame prince who inhabit

plain

plain countries: To live in hilly countries, requires more activity and vigour of body; the very moving from one place to another is laborious, the cold and blustering climates found in them, contribute to bracing up the human body, and to make it hardy. It is the same effect as is seen in cold climates, compared with hot ones, in whatever parts of the world they may be found. After the mountains are passed that separate the two countries, I went through a great extent of forest, and marsh land, very little of which is cultivated; and not much of it would pay for culture, unless the country in general was richer than it is.

Olmutz is a small but very well built city, prettily situated on the little river Moravia. It is a strong place both by nature and art; so that the King of Prussia, when he made the famous irruption into Moravia, and laid siege to it, did not seem to have had good intelligence of the state of the town, or the garrison. The streets are regular and well paved, and there are many good houses in it; the only publick buildings of any note, are the Jesuits college, the bishop's palace, and the town-house; the market place is surrounded by several well built houses. It is an agreeable town, and the inhabitants seem to be a very sociable people,

people, with more activity and industry, than is to be found among the Bohemians. Provisions are very cheap here: I lived at the Emprefs's Arms inn, two days, upon exceeding good fish and fowl, and good Hungarian wine, and when I paid my reckoning, I found that six shillings went to the full, as far as a guinea in England. Beef is only three half pence a pound; mutton is sometimes sold at a penny; and a fat turkey is to be bought for fourteen pence.

The 21st I left Olmutz, and proceeded to Brinn, the distance thirty miles, through a much more fertile country than north of Olmutz; it is better peopled, and much more of it cultivated: They do not sow much wheat here, but a great deal of rye, barley, peale, and beans; and the crops in general, carried a good appearance; they keep great herds of cattle, feeding them in winter on cabbages, turneps, and straw; all the latter, which they give to their cattle, they cut almost as small as chaff, with an engine made on purpose; very different from the chaff-cutter used in England. They chop the turneps, or cabbages into small pieces, and give them with chopt straw, and find that they go much the farther, and nourish the cattle much better. I never heard of any thing of this sort being

being practised in England; yet I should apprehend that it could not fail of answering extremely; it is certainly much worth the trial. They have vast herds of swine, which find their own subsistance in woods, and swampy grounds for most part of the year. They fatten them on beans, pease, and potatoes, which they cultivate on purpose: selling great quantities of bacon to Vienna, &c.

Brinn is well situated on the confluence of two rivers, and is reckoned the strongest place in Moravia; it has a castle that is very strong; the Austrians have usually a good garrison here; several new fortifications have been added both to this place, and to Olmutz since the last war, which I suppose were occasioned by the King of Prussia's bold march into this country, which alarmed them excessively at Vienna. There are about six thousand inhabitants in Brinn; the streets are narrow and crooked, but many of the houses very well built, and some of the publick edifices make a tolerable appearance, particularly the Jesuits college, and the churches of St. James, and St. Thomas.

The 22d I reached Laba, a little town thirty miles from Brinn; the country between them is better than the preceding; has less waste land, fewer forests and marshes; and the

the arable land beyond comparifon better cultivated. This is in a great meafure owing to the attention given to hufbandry-improvements by the court of Vienna. They were at the expence fome years ago, of bringing feveral Flemifh farmers from the country, between Oftend and Bruges; three of them were fettled in this country, being fupplied with all forts of implements, cattle, houfes, land, &c. by the Emprefs Queen, and fixed upon fome wafte, but very fertile lands belonging to the crown. They have had a large fucceffion of Moravian peafants, regularly working under them, in order to be inftructed in the Flemifh hufbandry; who being difcharged when frefh ones are taken, have much fpread feveral excellent cuftoms, and will in all probability, much improve the agriculture of the greateft part of the province. The effect has already been very confiderable; for though thefe Flemings do not occupy a thoufand acres of land in all, yet their methods already fpread over a country near fifteen miles long; all the hufbandry of which is by their means much improved. They have introduced clover here, which turns out one of the moft beneficial crops that can be fown; they have alfo made this culture of clover a preparation for wheat, fo that they have almoft entirely

banifhed

banished the custom of fallowing for wheat; which was the common method in Moravia. Spurry they also brought with them, with which they feed cows. To them likewise the Moravians are indebted for a much more systematic management of manure, than what they formerly followed: They form composts of dung, rotten vegetables, vast quantities of leaves, swept up on purpose in the open forests, turf, ashes, and other materials, which they mix together several times, and spread upon their clover fields—and on their cabbage grounds: They have also made them abundantly more attentive in keeping all their crops clear from weeds and in good order, by hoeing and weeding; all the cabbages I saw in this district, which has been profited thus from the example of the Flemings, were in very fine order, both in respect to pulverized soil, and a clearness from weeds.

I saw the castle of baron Skulitz, who had been extremely attentive in spreading this good Flemish husbandry. He resides constantly on his estate, and makes agriculture not only his business, but also his amusement: Immediately on their exhibiting a culture, superior to the old management of the Moravians, he followed it with so much intelligence and spirit, that he has advanced the value

lue of his eftate confiderably: He entered prefently into all their views, and introduced the beft hufbandry of the Auftrian provinces upon his own lands. Falling into difcourfe on the road with one of his bailiffs, he pointed out to me feveral large tracks of land, which not long ago were entirely wafte, but are now by this worthy nobleman's attention, better cultivated than moft of the province. He has introduced various new branches of hufbandry, which anfwer better than common crops; among thefe, hops and faffron he brought from Bohemia; madder from Silefia; and he raifes both hemp and flax in large quantities: All thefe crops he is remarkably attentive to, and gives them fuch uncommon fair play, that his firft trials, contrary to what is generally met with, turned out greatly fuccefsful, from whence he has been induced to continue them ever fince, and greatly to enlarge all his plantations of them, by which, and various other means, he has improved his revenues in a furprizing manner.

The owners of extenfive landed eftates, in poor countries, have all fuch an opportunity of increafing their income; and it is very amazing they do not oftener take advantage of it. If, like the nobleman here mentioned,

they

they would reside upon their estates, instead of spending all their time in the capital, squandering their revenues in a gulf of luxury, the measure of which is never full, and which cannot fail of impoverishing them, and bringing them into the most slavish dependence upon the will of the court; if they would act thus, they would find money flow into their coffers in a far greater abundance than they can ever hope to receive from the smiles of ministers; at the same time that they would reside where a shilling goes as far as a pound. In the profusion of a capital, the greatest estates are spent without making any unusual figure; but in the country, half the income would enable them to build and furnish costly palaces, and raise whole cities around them to be witnesses of their splendor. —I have, in the course of my travels, met with several instances, which shew, in the clearest light, the enjoyment and undoubted happiness which this kind of life confers, even upon noblemen, whose rank and revenue would allow them all the amusements of any metropolis. It is a most happy thing to any country, when a sovereign gives all the encouragement in his power to promote this rural attention in nobles, which cannot fail

of

of turning out highly beneficial to the whole community.

The 23d I got to Vienna, which is five-and-twenty miles from Laba, through a country that is very unequal, part of it being very rich, populous, and well cultivated, and much of it hilly, wild, and to appearance barren. In the cultivated tracks are many noblemen's feats; and the hufbandry around them is vifibly much better than elfewhere, which is owing to their drawing the peafants, as it were, into a ftring around them. They plant great quantities of faffron, which they reckon the moft profitable crop they have: they have alfo plenty of good crops of wheat and barley; and their extenfive meadows and paftures feed large herds of cattle, which from the neighbourhood of Vienna turn to very good account. I faw feveral crops of the turnep cabbage for cattle. But hufbandry fuffers much in all this country, and indeed through moft parts of Germany, for want of inclofures: they might eafily make them, and at a fmall expence, but neglect the work entirely, which muft be for want of fully underftanding the advantages of them: Indeed, labour is of fo little value, that every fort of cattle has always a keeper with them, tho' the herd is ever so small, yet corn and saffron often suffer.

Vienna is situated on the south side of the Danube, but has not the advantage of that great river running through it; for it stands on a small branch of it, there being several islands formed here, by the river dividing itself. If the suburbs are included, it is a very large city, but within the walls and fortifications it is only three miles in circumference. It is regularly fortified, but has so few outworks, as to be a place of small strength, and only defended by a small army. At the siege in 1683, the Turks shewed themselves to be extremely ignorant in the art of conducting such an enterprize; and their engineers were miserable ones, else they might have taken the city some time before the King of Poland raised the siege; and had that event happened, Hungary had now been in possession of the Ottomans.

Vienna within the walls makes a most inelegant appearance, from the narrowness of the streets. I am one who would not give sixpence for a fine building, if there is not a sufficient area to view it from. The English boast of the church of St. Paul's at London; and will sometimes assert it equal to St. Peter's at Rome; but if it were doubly finer, I should prefer

prefer St Peter's, from the opportunity one has of viewing it; and the area around a great building, ought to be so much esteemed a part of it, as to be criticised with it; and the architect's abilities called in question for faults in it, as much as if he blundered in the proportion of the cupola. Thus in Vienna, there are many palaces (of which I had read and heard much,) in streets as narrow as old Bristol; and at the same time all the houses are five, six, seven, and some of them eight stories high; and it is said, they have almost as many stories of cellars under ground, as of floors above. Formerly all the windows were grated with iron bars like prisons, from the street to the upper floor, and vast numbers of houses are so now, but I see it is left off in the principal palaces.

The imperial palace is a structure that will answer to none that sees it; it consists of several courts, surrounded with irregular buildings; though, notwithstanding some late additions, it makes but a very mean appearance; the apartments are neither spacious, nor furnished in the manner one would expect, for a court long famed as one of the most expensive in Europe. The library is supposed to rank among the first in Europe; the number of volumes

volumes are not lefs than ninety thoufand; and the collection of manufcripts, fuppofed to be extremely valuable. I was fhewn feveral great curiofities, but upon thefe occafions there never is time allowed for any ufeful examination, and if there were, it would fignify little to the unlearned in the oriental tongues, in which the moft valuable manufcripts are written.

Many of the palaces of the nobility, are moft magnificent ftructures; that of the great Eugene with his famous library and collections I had moft pleafure in viewing; the Mansfield palace, and that of count Daun, are alfo great edifices, with feveral others, in which the painting, gilding, carving, and furniture are as rich as poffible.

The univerfity of Vienna, is very famous in Germany and Hungary; the number of ftudents is confiderable, and they have good accommodations for thofe of fortune, and many valuable privileges.

There is not much worth feeing in the churches of Vienna; the cathedral is the principal, and it is a large building; but nothing is uncommon in it but the heighth of its fpire, which, fince Strafburg, is become French, is the higheft in the empire. The Jefuits church is a fine building; and the convents of
Carmelites,

Carmelites, Francifcans, Benedictines, and
Auftin Friars, are vifited by thofe who take
any delight in viewing thefe fort of buildings;
for my part, I have an averfion at feeing fuch
ufelefs edifices filled with tribes of pernicious
orders of lazy priefts, who do nothing to gain
their livelihood, but are maintained by the
induftry of every body elfe: It is amazing,
that Roman catholick princes do not find out
that every monk in their dominions might be
a foldier, without the country fuffering a
whit the more: and in many cafes the foldier would pay well for his maintenance; but
as to the monk, he is fubfifted in the moft
unufeful of all fpecies of idlenefs.—But there
are other inftances of the catholick piety of
Vienna, befides her monks and nuns; in one
of the fquares, is a very large and coftly ftatue of the Trinity, reprefenting the Deity
clafping Chrift in his arms, and the Holy
Ghoft hovering over them. This was erected
by the Emperor Leopold, inftead of an eque-
ftrian ftatue, which in other cities would
have been erected to the fovereign. To this
famous piece of folly, all the Roman catholicks bow as they pafs. Religious prejudices
fhould certainly be laid afide by all travellers;
but is it poffible for a man of fenfe not to rejoice, that education has not enflaved him to

an obfervance of, or veneration for fuch mummery? In many inftances, religion makes Roman catholick countries extremely difagreeable to travel through.

I brought feveral letters of recommendation to Vienna, to perfons from whofe converfation, I expected fome valuable information concerning the general ftate of all the Auftrian dominions at prefent, in refpect of agriculture, manufactures, commerce, revenues, and military power; but I was ftrangely difappointed: there is a haughty referve in every man of the leaft confequence here, which not only precludes any information of this fort; but at the fame time renders a refidence in any but a publick character very difagreeable at Vienna. But after all my letters had failed, that is, introduced me only to people who thought that I had no bufinefs with any thing but eating, drinking, going to court, and playing at cards, a life by no means agreeable to me; after this I fell accidentally into company with a field-officer in their fervice, a native of Milan: this gentleman was extremely communicative, very fenfible, and had travelled often through moft of the dominions of the Emprefs Queen. He gave me a very rational, and candid account of things, as appeared by his manner, and the

the confirmations I had afterwards from several persons in other parts of Europe. To agriculture this gentleman had not at all attended; he could give me no more account of its general state in the countries he had been in, than with that of the moon. I found from him however, that the manufactures which have lately been established in Hungary, flourish very much; the Empress Queen, and her ministers, have long been eager to cloath her troops with her subjects manufactures; instead of selling all their wool unmanufactured. Hungary, as well as Austria, Bohemia, and Moravia, feed many sheep, especially Hungary, a great part of which is a continued and fertile sheep-walk. Great numbers of Hungarians have been set to work upon this wool; and weavers, spinners, reelers, &c. brought from Flanders, to teach the natives to work it; and many of them have proved very docile in learning: so that at present, woollen goods are made to the amount of near an hundred thousand pounds a year, which is a very great thing in Hungary—where, before these exertions, were no manufactures at all—They are established in most of the populous towns of that kingdom; and if they are brought, to employ the poor people in them, who have no other employment,

ployment, it will be an immense acquisition, and save the export of very great sums of money. As to trade, the inland situation of the Austrian dominions, is such as allows of very little foreign commerce. Attempts were made at Triest, but they were so languid, and suffered such interruptions during the war, that the commerce of the port is yet nothing that deserves mention; notwithstanding that an active prince, liberal in useful expence, and attentive to such improvements, might have made Triest the seat of a considerable commerce; but all these circumstances have been wanting.

The revenues of the dominions of the house of Austria, are considerable; the following account of them was given to this gentleman, by a person who had many opportunities of being well informed.

Bohemia	£ 700,000
Moravia	190,000
Hungary	400,000
Austria	400,000
Transilvania	50,000
Sclavonia and Croatia	100,000
Stria, Curinthia, and Carniola	200,000
Tyroll, Brixen, Trent	160,000
The countries of Swabia	20,000

The

The Netherlands ——— 150,000
Milan, and Mantua ——— 400,000
Tuscany ——— ——— 500,000

Total ——— ——— £ 3,270,000

What degree of accuracy there is in this table; I am not able to ascertain, but from the information I have received from other hands, I believe the total to be near the truth: but Tuscany must not be reckoned: the common idea at Vienna coincides with these particulars; which makes the Imperial revenue near three millions: though there are some sanguine politicians, who insist on it's amounting to five; but that is much exaggerated. The revenues of all these countries might be very much improved; nobody doubts but a better system of taxation, and a more œconomical collection would raise five millions, with very near as much ease to the people as three at present; but the lower classes of the people throughout most of these dominions are miserably fleeced, and pillaged, while the nobility escape with paying a much less proportion than they ought. The Netherlands might in particular yield a very considerable revenue, and prove the finest and most profitable provinces

vinces belonging to the houfe of Auftria; but in order to that, great changes fhould be made in the conftitutions of the cities; manufactures fhould receive encouragement, and commerce be re-eftablifhed in the ports; all which might be eafily done, and the revenues of the fovereign become wonderfully improved; whereas at prefent they yield no more than might be expected if they were fituated no better than Auftria, or Moravia, inftead of being the fineft fpot in Europe, in every refpect; and inhabited by a people naturally as induftrious as any in the world. Flanders, fince the Dutch were mafters of the navigation of Antwerp has wanted a port; but Oftend, for an hundred thoufand pounds, might be made as good a one as any in Europe for merchantmen.

The many improvements, which have been talked of by the court of Vienna for the hereditary dominions, in agriculture, manufactures, and commerce, were they put in execution, would at the fame time much improve the revenue, and in a manner free the country of thofe evils, which ufually flow from increafing the publick income of a crown. But there is a dilatorinefs and a languor in every thing tranfacted at this court, even in its own moft intricate concerns, that damp the fpirit of all improvement, so that any object of this sort, upon a moderate computation, will be talked of half a century, before it is executed; this was the case with the establishment of the woollen manufacture in Hungary, and with every thing else: so that it is not thought the Austrian revenues, however they would admit of it, will for a long time be put upon a better footing than they are, or have any other improvements than what results from oppressing the lower classes of the people still more : than which no measure can give a greater stab to all general national improvements. Was the King of Prussia possessed of the Austrian dominions in exchange for his own, we should soon see them make a very different appearance; he would raise much greater revenues, with far greater ease to the people; and would throw such a vigour into all the transactions which the possession of Flanders, and the Italian dominions would introduce him to, that the importance of them would speedily appear in a very different light from what they do at present.

The great object of attention at Vienna, is the army; this is so far reprehensible in politicks, as it encreases the necessity of laying a foundation previous to every superstructure: it is the revenue that pays and supports the army, and

and all increase of the latter must depend on a foregoing increase of the former: to raise a great revenue is much more essential, than to raise a great army; but the soldiers have a peculiar faculty of swallowing up a revenue, they have none at creating it. That prince therefore, who would be truly formidable, should attend to the prosperity of his income, before he thinks of greatly increasing his troops.

The following are the particulars of the present standing forces of the house of Austria. I insert them on the same authority as the above paper of the revenue; believing from other information which I have received, that it is near the truth; though I should remark, that all lists of armies are apt to exceed the reality, rather than fall beneath it.

	Men.
Dragoons	23,846
Curiassers	16,000
Hussars, and Croats	14,640
Hunters	6,300
Free troops	8,000
Infantry	164,386
Artillery	2,800
Total	235,972

GERMANY.

The whole army, whatever the total may be, is certainly in excellent order; the regiments full, and well officered, their cloathing regularly delivered, their arms much better than ever; the artillery very numerous; and no expence has been spared in forming engineers; the magazines of ammunition and all sorts of military stores, full, and in good order: these attentions have occupied the court ever since the peace, and they have been indefatigable in them. Now, that all these particulars are compleated, they are employed in repairing all the fortifications in Bohemia, Moravia, Auftria, Hungary, and Transilvania; new ones are in some places erecting, and many old ones greatly improved; this is a work of immense expence, and consequently it goes on slowly. In every one of these particulars, the Austrians strength is greater than at the breaking out of the last war. I before remarked, that the case was the same with the King of Prussia. These potentates are certainly jealous of each other; but I believe in no respect that threatens a fresh war: but the state of affairs in other parts, makes it necessary for them to be strongly armed. The aspect of affairs in Pruffia and Poland, fills the house of Auftria with uneasiness; and although Pruffia espouses in her manifestos the same cause in Polish affairs as the

the Ruffian Emprefs, ftill it can only be, becaufe the power of that empire is too great for him to break with. Moft certainly the increafe of the formidablenefs of Ruffia, ought in good politicks to fill both Pruffia, and Auftria with the deepeft jealoufy; future alliances with it, in cafe of a new war in Germany, muft be very uncertain; and againft whoever fhe declares, her weight will probably fall too heavy to be refifted. The opportunity of the war between the Ruffians and Turks, has generally been taken by the Auftrians for attacking the Porte: fuch a meafure now would infure the reftoration of Belgrade and Servia, and perhaps yet greater advantages; but not making ufe of it, may be owing to two reafons: firft, in return for the Turks not playing the fame game when the Emprefs Queen was at war with Pruffia; and fecondly, becaufe fuch a conduct would give greater advantages to the arms of Ruffia, than the houfe of Auftria wifhes to fee.

CHAPTER X.

Journey from Vienna through Austria—Description of the Archdutchy—Bavaria—Munich—Revenues and forces.—

JULY 1st, I left Vienna, and that day travelled forty miles to St. Poltu, through a very various country. Near Vienna, it is very gay, being lightly adorned with villas, which have extensive gardens, and planted groves about them, but all in a miserable taste. I stopped to view one pretty near the road, which the postilions told me belonged to a great nobleman at court; a description of the ground before the house will give a tolerable idea of the taste most prevalent here in ornamenting their country seats. A canal with a small bridge over it in the center, parted the area before the house from the road; from the bridge to the house door was about a hundred yards; a broad stone-way led from one to the other; on each side ranged in exact order a statue, an urn, and a cross interchangeably; these were on a slip of grass: on the other side two canals nicely laid out, like the former, by rule, and at each corner of the three, a statue. The ground on each side was formed

into

into a grafs-plot, furrounded by a parterre of flowers, and in the center of each plot, a fmall fountain. From thefe particulars of the approach to a rural villa, all unfeen may be very exactly guefled; and it evidently appears that the Auftrians are at leaft one hundred years behind us in the art of gardening. It is the fame with the French, and all the other nations of Europe. In fome gardens I was fhewn when in Italy, before I was told that they were executed in imitation of nature, upon the plan of my countryman Brown, whofe fame had reached there; and it is not eafy to be conceived how ridiculous every thing was; the leaft deviations from line and compafs work, amidft a great deal of it, were efteemed exertions in the art of imitating nature. A more ridiculous jumble was never feen; much worfe than thofe made purely artificial.

Ornamenting a piece of ground, in the manner of our great gardener, and in the tafte yet fuperior, in which fome private gentlemen in England have laid out their grounds, is an art that requires genius, and more attention than will ever be given to it, in countries where they refide ten months out of the twelve in the capital, and very many, the other two alfo: where this is the cafe, the expence will not be fpared, which we fee in every thing that relates

lates to the country; no article about a nobleman while he refides in the country in England, but what infinitely exceeds the fame with any foreign nobleman of equal fortune. Their wealth is all expended upon their town houfes, and their town refidence; it is not therefore to be wondered at any more, that the Englifh have not fuch fine palaces in London, as that the French and Italians have not fuch fine country feats.

Thefe forty miles do not exhibit an agriculture that is very flourifhing; yet the country is not much in want of people, for the towns and villages are thick. The foil is in general very good; but they do not feem to have any ideas of cultivating it with neatnefs; wild fhrubbery grounds are fuffered to break into the corn, in ragged borders, and fmall wafte fpots, where the plough, upon account of fome hillock, or hole, does not go, are left covered with weeds, to blow all over their fallows; they have no idea of cleaning fuch fpots by way of prevention, and fuch numbers of them, as I faw in this day's journey, would not be met with in half an Englifh county. They fow large quantities of faffron, which they reckon a profitable culture, an acre yielding a produce of about three pounds, if the crop is good. There are many vineyards, but the wine fells fo badly, that they affured me, corn and faffron ſtand in general much better; and they do not confine their vines to tracks improper for ploughing.

Wheat, barley, rye, peafe and beans, are commonly cultivated, but no oats; the crops are but midling. Turneps, turnep cabbages, cabbages, and potatoes, are cultivated in large quantities; the former for cattle, and the potatoes for fattening hogs, for which they boil them. They have large herds of fwine, which feed all fummer long in the woods, many of which are extenſive. Horned cattle are alfo very plentiful here, and as they houſe them in the winter, they raiſe large quantities of dung, which ought to enfure a much better hufbandry than theirs. I paffed a fmall farm, near St. Poltu, that was cut out of a wafte, and to appearance a barren common, on the ſide of a large hill; difpofed into ten fields by beautiful quick hedges, which put me in mind of the beft cultivated part of England: the incloſures rifing one above another, on the ſide of the hill, were feen diſtinctly from the road; they were covered with various crops, which appeared much fuperior to thofe of the cultivated parts of the country I had paffed; the houſe was fmall, but extremely neat. As foon as I had looked attentively at this very agreeable fight, I was going

ing to make up to it; but recollecting that I should be in the dark, I determined to go on to the stage, and come next morning to view that farm, which seemed a creation in the midst of a desart.

I accordingly put my intention in execution, the morning of the 2d, and returned about three miles to the place, and asking for the master of it, he appeared immediately; a fine tall open countenanced soldier, in an old suit of regimentals. I desired to see his farm, upon which he very readily walked with me into it. I went through all the ten inclosures; the hedges were regularly planted, and had each of them a ditch; the gates were all in good order, and every thing carried an appearance of neatness, most uncommon in Germany. He had three meadows, each of them watered by a small stream he had brought from the hill above his farm; it filled a little pond for watering the cattle, and might be conducted at pleasure in the proper season, over all parts of the fields for manuring them, which he practises in winter and spring. He had a field of wheat, another of barley, two of clover, and three of turneps and cabbages; and his fields were all much of the same size, being each about six English acres. Turneps and cabbages he grew on his fallow for cleaning the land; succeeded them with barley, and then took clover, upon which he sows his wheat. This husbandry, which nearly resembles the best of Flanders, surprized me in the midst of Austria, where nothing of the kind is to be found. He keeps a dairy of cows; a small flock of sheep on the neighbouring waste, and oxen for ploughing and carting; he houses all his cattle in winter; his sheep every night in sheep houses; and litters every thing well with fern, which he cuts upon the waste. He is extremely attentive to raising large quantities of dung, which he manages by keeping as many cattle as he possibly can, and by mixing turf, and virgin earth with his dung as the cattle make it all winter long; by this means he is enabled to manure three fields, or eighteen acres very richly every year; but what gives a virtue to his dunghill, superior to any thing else is his bringing all the human ordure away from the little town of Poltu, for which, some of the inhabitants ignorant of its value, give a trifle for taking it away; he is at the expence of cleaning all the necessaries there, and of carting it to his farm; he mixes it up with his dung and virgin earth, and assures me that it forms the richest compost in the world; all the manure he raises in this manner, being applied to his turnep and cabbage grounds, he gets

gets prodigious crops of thofe vegetables; and I remarked that they were kept perfectly free from weeds by hoeing: his cabbages are all planted in regular rows on ridges, and the fpaces between the rows ploughed feveral times while growing, as well to kill the weeds as to keep the land in good tillage, all which appeared to me to be an excellent fyftem. His crops of wheat yield four quarters an acre; his barley five, his clover gives four tons of hay at two mowings; and his turneps and cabbages maintain a vaft flock: an acre of the former he reckons fufficient to winter-feed two oxen or cows; one of cabbages will winter three or four; but the expences of them are higher. All thefe crops I fuppofe are equal to the beft cultivated parts of England.

Upon returning to his houfe he gave me his hiftory. He was a corporal in a regiment of foot, quartered, during fix years; in Flanders, and Brabant, where, as he had always a ftrong bent towards hufbandry, he remarked very minutely their practices, and often worked in the fields for Flemifh farmers. Upon the war breaking out with the king of Pruffia, he was early in that fervice, and made a ferjeant, in which capacity he behaved fo much to Marfhal Daun's fatisfaction at the battle of Hockchirken, in fight of him, that he gave him promises upon the spot, of promotion; but these were not thought of afterwards, till being represented by another person to the Empress Queen, and allowed by count Daun, she personally asked him in the presence of the whole court, if he had any particular request to make: upon which he asked his discharge, and a piece of this waste to cultivate, being born in the parish. It was granted at once; and further, his sovereign built him the house and offices directly, and gave him an hundred pounds to stock the farm with. With this small beginning he went to work directly, and in nine years has raised every thing to the state I saw. His industry is unbounded: though a continued success has attended all his undertakings, and his crops prove as fine as possible, bringing him in large sums of money, yet he continues to work with the same severity as ever, and does much the greatest part of all the business of his farm with his own hands; he has a son about twenty-five who executes the rest. The Empress has been twice to see him, and expressed the highest approbation of his conduct, and made him a handsome present. His methods have been put in execution under his own direction upon the estates of two noblemen in the neighbourhood, and with good success; so that this

worthy

worthy foldier is like to be of more benefit to his country than half a dozen generals; and shews that nothing is of more importance than to eftablifh such examples as thefe in various parts of a dominion : for although they may fpread flowly, yet they certainly will fpread, and that they cannot do without being of very great public benefit.

By night, I reached a little town called Munfbery, being half way to Lintz, at the diftance of thirty miles from Poltu, through a country that is cultivated in a very different manner from the foldier's farm I had left, whofe name (by the way) is Picco. The crops are in general bad and very full of weeds; and they feem to plough the foil very badly, although their ploughs are drawn by fix oxen, and they have two men, or a man and a lad to drive them, with another man to hold the plough; it is evident from this that the price of labour is low, or the farmer, that is the nobility, could not allow fuch a fuperfluity of hands; but while the time of the peafants belongs to their lords, without any pay, fuch inftances will be very common; but the whole fyftem makes a very different figure from my friend Picco's, whofe farm is a contraft to the whole archdutchy. They cultivate many hops, faffron, and vines, and thefe articles exhauft all their lands

lands applied to common husbandry, of the dung which they ought to have, without yielding a return proportioned. Picco, when I asked him why he did not cultivate these articles, assured me that none of them equalled common crops in profit, provided the latter were managed in the manner they ought to be; and of this I have no doubt, for all these uncommon articles require a great deal of attention, and an infinity of labour, especially vines, while the produce is of such a bad sort, that the returns are inconsiderable. Near Lintz, the country improves much, being in itself finely variegated with hills and dales, wood and water; it is also better cultivated; there is a very little waste land, and many seats of the nobility are scattered about it, attracted I suppose by the agreeableness of the country.

Lintz is extremely well situated on the banks of the Danube: It is small, well built, and a neat place; the streets well paved, and kept very clean. What sets off the buildings in an unusual manner, is the materials of which they are raised; being a white stone that preserves its colour. The market-place is large and handsome; and is adorned with two fountains. The Empress has a palace here, well furnished, which from an high situation overlooks the course of the Danube very

beautifully;

beautifully; she used to come here often, but has not of late years. The Jesuits college is one of the best buildings in the place, and the library has the reputation of being remarkably well chosen. This place is the capital of upper Austria; for the states assemble no where else. For its size, it is very populous, which is owing to some manufactures they have that are flourishing; particularly that of woollen goods, and of silk and worsted; also gun-barrels, for which they are famous. The wool they work up is that of Austria, and much comes from Bohemia; all these fabricks employ six or seven hundred hands.

The 5th I got to Newberg in Bavaria, the distance forty miles. This line of country is all very agreeable; from the inequalities of the ground, and its open groves, with many rivers; nor is it wanting in numerous little towns and villages, the neighbourhood of the Danube drawing many inhabitants, by the constant trade carried on upon it; and by the numerous boats, barges, sloops, &c. which pass and repass upon all sorts of business. I observed hops, saffron, and vines were common culture, and some flax, which is made into coarse linnens in the neighbouring towns. Newberg is a little place, but very well built, and remarkably clean,. The Elector Palatine is sovereign of the dutchy, of which it is the capital;

capital and, has a small palace here, which however contains nothing worth seeing. The Jesuits church is the best publick edifice in the place. The only trade of Newberg is wine; but very little of it is good; several sorts are sold so cheap as three halfpence a quart.

The 6th I reached Muldorf, the distance fifty miles, through a very fine, populous, and well cultivated country, being part of the Electorate of Bavaria. There seems through this line of country, to be more industry, activity and happiness, than in any I had passed for a long while, and yet the peasants are in a state of villainage as well as elsewhere, but they are treated in a kinder manner; have more property and better houses; and many of them are also farmers, who by industry and frugality have saved money; and find out the means of disposing of it to good advantage. Much of this country is enclosed, than which there cannot be any improvement of so much consequence; and the present Elector has given many privileges and encouragements to all who enclose their farms, as well as exempting them from antient customs and rights, which were extremely injurious to open lands. There are many vineyards in this country, and the wine is better than that of Austria. Sheep seem to be a principal article in their husbandry; they keep great numbers, and of a better breed

breed than common; which I am told was originally owing to procuring some rams from Flanders. They yield large fleeces, and there are many manufactories for working up the wool, which receive great encouragement from the government. Every farm of any size, (that is, every division of an estate that is under a distinct steward or bailiff) has a large sheep-house, with a roof, but open on one side to the south; in this house they fold their sheep every night the whole year round, and depend on it principally for manuring their lands: when they begin to fold, they spread over the floor light virgin soil, turf, sand, or peat earth, and fold upon it till it is very moist and dirty; then they make a fresh layer, and so go on; but to every eighteen inches of depth, (for they remove the heap but once a year) they litter with straw; and in extreme wet or snowy weather they do the same. This is upon the whole an excellent system for raising manure, and is a Flemish custom, though with one or two variations: but I should think the sheep lying upon such a dunghill, would be prejudicial to their health; however, the Bavarians assert the contrary, and say that the health of the animal does not suffer in the least; and that the wool is much better than it would be if the sheep were exposed to the weather.

Muldorf

Muldorf is a little town, agreeably fituated, and regularly fortified, but it is not a place of any great ftrength; the ftreets are broad, ftrait, and well built, and the market-place fpacious, and furrounded with feveral buildings that are a great ornament to it. There are feveral churches and convents, but none that contain any thing remarkable.

The 7th I got to Munich, the diftance feven and thirty miles, and the country agreeable and well cultivated; there are many more nobility who refide conftantly on their lands in this country, than in any I have feen in Germany; and to this I attribute the advantage of the fuperior cultivation: for as the nobles are the farmers, it is no wonder that eftates there are managed better under the mafter's eye, than in his abfence. Although there are not many of them that are proficients in agriculture, yet a life paffed in the midft of its bufinefs, muft yield a greater knowledge of its circumftances than one which is entirely employed in the parade of a court. Befides, there can be little doubt but the nobles themfelves treat their peafants better than the race of bailiffs, agents, &c. who ufually oppress and fqueeze them the more, in order to have the better opportunity of enriching themfelves; and I find it evident, wherever I have been in Germany, that the landlords are the richeft,

and

and their eftates the beft cultivated, where the peafants are allowed fome degree of liberty and property. The happier that race of people, the better for the nobles; the latter will not in all cafes be brought to believe this, but nothing admits of clearer proof.

Their corn through this track of country looked very well; and I obferved particularly, that their fallows intended for next year were well ploughed, and clean; whereas they are full of weeds in many parts of Germany, and much fuch bad management as I had feen in Auftria. The foil here is a rich loam, with fome light tracks: they plough chiefly with oxen. They fallow their lands for wheat; and then fow barley; after the barley, they take peafe or buck-wheat, and then turneps, or cabbages; but they do not fow any clover, which the Auftrian foldier, and all Flanders and Brabant find fo profitable. Wheat yields two quarters and an half per acre, barley three, and buck-wheat four; and their turneps and cabbages are applied to feeding their cattle and fheep; but all are houfed in winter.

Munich I think without exception, the fineft city in Germany; Drefden, while in its grandeur, I am told furpaffed it; and fome parts of Berlin are very beautiful, and al things confidered, they now yield to this place. Itis fituated on the river Ifer; which dividing into several channels, waters all parts of the town: so that little streams run through many of the streets, confined in stone channels, which has a most clean and agreeable effect. The streets, squares, and courts are spacious, and airy; which sets off all the buildings much, and makes them appear finer than others much more costly in other cities. The streets in particular, are so strait, that many of them intersect each other at right-angles, and are very broad, and extremely well built. There are sixteen churches and monasteries in it, many of them very handsome edifices; these with the electoral palace, and other publick ings, take up near half the city: so that it may easily be supposed the place is in general very well built.

The principal of all these publick edifices, is the electoral palace, which is rather a convenient than an elegant building. It is very large; having four courts in it, and all of them large, but there is a want of finishing in the insides of all the places in Germany, that cannot fail disgusting an Englishman, who has been used to see the houses of the nobility in his own country finished to the garrets, as compleatly as a snuff-box; and certainly it is a most agreeable circumstance. In the palace of Munich, the finest room, which is the grand hall, being an hundred and eighteen feet long

long by fifty two broad, is open to the roof, so as entirely to destroy the effect which would result from such a size if finished: birds fly about in it as in a barn, and drop their favours on the heads of the company as they pass. I have in Germany seen many instances of unfinishing equal to this. There is a great profusion of marble in the several apartments, but it is not wrought in an agreeable manner. The furniture is in general old; it has been very rich, but has nothing in it striking; nor is the collection of pictures comparable to many others in Germany. The Museum is well filled with many curiosities; of which as Keysler gives a list, I shall therefore say no more of them.—The Jesuits college is among the finest buildings belonging to the church: it is very spacious. The great church, and the Franciscans monastery, are also worth seeing; the latter order is possessed of very great revenues. Several palaces of the nobility make a very good figure, and the town-house is better than many I have seen. The number of inhabitants is computed at fifty thousand.

The palaces most worth seeing are the Elector's country ones of Sleisheim and Nymphenburg, near Munich. Sleisheim is a fine building, and much better finished than that of Munich; the portico supported by marble pillars is fine; in the apartments, which are

furnished

furnished in an agreeable manner, is a very good collection of pictures, but they are chiefly by Flemish masters. Nymphenburg exhibits the German taste of gardening in perfection; the Bavarians holding them to be the finest in the empire; the situation, wood, and water would admit of something beautiful, but here is nothing but the old-fashioned fountains, statues, monsters, &c.

It is thought by most persons at Munich, as well as in other parts of Germany, the electorate of Bavaria has thoroughly recovered the mischiefs it suffered in the war of 1744, and is now as rich and populous as ever. The electoral revenues are reckoned to amount to six hundred thousand pounds a year, and are improving: the standing army consists of eleven thousand foot, and three thousand horse; but the Bavarians say, their prince could bring forty thousand men into the field; however, it is certain that, if he could bring them there he could not maintain them, without their being in the pay of foreigners. While the house of Bavaria continues on good terms with that of Austria, there is no danger of its suffering by the electorate being again made the seat of war.

FINIS.

www.ingramcontent.com/pod-product-compliance
Lightning Source LLC
Chambersburg PA
CBHW030302240426
43673CB00040B/1027